Fern M

Hope you enjoy the
book.

Lowell + Sue
Smith

The
Benders
Keepers of the
Devil's Inn

THE
BENDERS

KEEPERS OF THE
DEVIL'S INN

by

Fern Morrow Wood

Copy Design and Illustration by Mike Wood
Copy Layout and Cover Layout by Kala Carter

The Benders: Keepers of the Devil's Inn
by Fern Morrow Wood

Published May, 1992

Second Printing March, 1993

ISBN 0-9606922-1-5.

Library of Congress Catalog Card Number: 92 - 90636

Printed by BookCrafters
Chelsea, Michigan

DEDICATION

This book is dedicated to the memory of the Benders' victims. Some of their names were never known; others have been forgotten. Their blood cries out for vengeance — or, at least, remembrance.

PREFACE

My interest in the Bender case stemmed from volunteer work at the Cherryvale Museum. I am indebted to all of those writers who set down their information and impressions in years gone by, to the journalists whose words are preserved in the microfilm department of the Kansas Historical Society, to my dear friend Gene DeGruson for the introduction, to friends and acquaintances who responded to pleas for more facts, to Kala Carter for expert and patient layout work, to my family who gave constant support, and to Kerri for typing, Mike for cover design, Toni for editing, and Leonard for chauffeuring.

INTRODUCTION

Despite biblical injunction, murder fascinates us more than any of the admirable but generally pale virtues. (The lives of the saints have little commercial value in the twentieth century.) By contrast, we seem never to get our fill of murder, especially if there is mystery involved. Unsolved murders perennially resurface in song, fiction, and folklore.

Angeline Crowell of Pittsburg, Kansas, for example, in all likelihood would now be all but forgotten if she had not been accused in 1955 of shooting her husband, William Woodward II. But as Ann Woodward, a small-town girl who married New York's most eligible bachelor, she became the model for a murderess in Truman Capote's <u>Answered Prayers</u> (serialized in <u>Esquire</u> in 1975), reappeared as the younger of <u>The Two Mrs. Grenvilles</u> in Dominick Dunne's best selling novel of 1986, and was portrayed a year later by Ann-Margret in a television miniseries based on that novel. She reemerged in the 1990's as the subject of a full-length biography by Susan Brady.

Mrs. Woodward, however, pales in contrast to other Kansas criminals, for if one murder excites, mass murder is much more intriguing. And the Sunflower State has had its share of those, too. Kansas will always be associated with the ruthless murder of the Clutter family in Holcomb because of Truman Capote's masterpiece, <u>In Cold Blood.</u> Seemingly never to be forgotten is the wholesale murder of the Sell family near Erie in 1886. But Kansas will perhaps be best remembered in the annals of murder for the somewhat dubious distinction of being the site of the nation's first serial killings.

These murders were perpetrated in the early 1870s by the four members of the so-called Bender family nine miles from Cherryvale. Thomas Brower Peacock of Independence wrote a poem about the Bender murders almost as soon as they were discovered; pulp novelists of the period wrote Bender novels by the score. No doubt influenced by the ensuing years of sensational writings on the subject, a Bender motion picture was filmed in Girard, Kansas, in 1939. The early days of television saw several dramatizations about the ghastly murders of Southeast Kansas. Manly Wade Wellman wrote A Candle of the Wicked in 1960, and Robert H. Alderman published another best-selling novel, The Bloody Benders, in 1970. There are undoubtedly other works-in-progress as this book is being published.

It is not the poetry and novels that you will find explored in this volume. Fern Morrow Wood early in her research became addicted to the facts surrounding the bloody career of the Benders and has assembled a chronological narrative, prefaced with a diary which details how she became entrapped by the family. She has sifted the reminiscences of long-forgotten neighbors for revelations; she has searched newspapers of the period and shares newly discovered documents; her skeptical eye examines the conclusions of previous chroniclers.

For those unfamiliar with the Bender story, perhaps the most concise introduction is the version collected by Vance Randolph, the midwestern folklorist, as he heard it from his grandfather, Farwell

Gould, in April 1930, who in turn recalled how it was told to him by friends who lived near South Coffeyville, Oklahoma, in the 1880s:

> One time there was a family that called theirself Bender, and they used to keep tavern up in Kansas. They was doing pretty good at it, too. But one day an old gentleman shot a Yankee right in front of the Bender place, and when some folks went to bury the Yankee in the back yard, they found pretty near forty men was buried there already. It was men that come to the tavern to stay all night, and the Benders had cut their throats and stole their money. So the Governor of Kansas offered a big reward for the Benders dead or alive, but all four of them got away and come down into the Territory.
>
> They stole some ponies in the Cherokee Nation, just about where Nowata is now, and started south. Old man Bender and his wife rode ahead, and then some Johnny and Katy. Them two was brother and sister, but they slept together just like they wasn't no kin. They didn't care who knowed it, either, and whenever she had a baby they would just knock it in the head. The Benders was not respectable people, and kind of tough. The folks that lived in the Territory didn't like them much, and they never asked the Benders to eat dinner with them, or come to the dances.
>
> There was gangs of men from Kansas riding round a-hunting the Benders, but

everybody says they never heard tell of them. The folks knowed them Yankees was just after the blood-money, and they didn't want no part in such doings. But one day a bunch of these Kansas fellows run onto the Benders unexpected, and they tied all four of them up with rope. The Benders had more than forty thousand dollars in money belts and a hatful of watches and jewelry. The Yankees was so tickled to get all this stuff that some of them wanted to turn the Benders loose. But while they was dividing up the money they got to fighting among themselves, and two of them was killed.

The rest of the Yankees was pretty drunk, and did not trust nobody. If they took the Benders back to get the reward, the law might try to take the forty thousand dollars away from them. And maybe they would have to answer questions about how them two fellows got killed. They figured it might be better to let the reward money go, and just divide up the Benders' stuff and not go back to Kansas at all. So finally they killed all four of the Benders, and buried the six corpses in a big hole under a bluff. Then each one of them fellows took his share of the money and jewelry and rode off by himself...

There are many versions of the above story, some put forth as eye witness accounts, each tailored to the teller's audience and ended according to the narrator's sense of dramatic justice. It is through tales such as this that Mrs. Wood has carved her way, discarding that which cannot be proved by contemporary evidence, but nevertheless following up on every clue as far as humanly possible. The result is fascinating. That some of the "facts" remain contradictory and the solution uncertain merely serve to whet our interest and make us want to know more. The mystery continues, but Fern Wood has provided an excellent road map to the Bender Hill mysteries.

Gene DeGruson
Curator of Special Collections
Pittsburg State University
Pittsburg, Kansas

Chapter 1

• ◄━━◄◉►━━► •

Tuesday, May 7, 1991

I am not a superstitious person — I have no fear of ghosts or evil spirits. Yet as I stepped through the gates of Harmony Grove Cemetery, my eye fell on the tombstone of Rudolph Brockman, and I felt an odd chilling of the blood. His name I had met many times in those long-ago accounts, and from this grave I sensed a strong emanation of evil. The old crumbling markers of that era jumped out at me as I walked — Father Dienst, who had spoken out at a school meeting, and William Dick, who was with his son LeRoy as all of the tragedy unfolded.

I drove north from the cemetery to Bender Mound and turned on the dirt road that led to the claims filed by Pa Bender and his alleged son, John. I was alone on this dirt road; the sky had turned brooding and threatening. I was not certain of the exact location of the inn. The green wheat gave no hint of any difference in the soil, yet I was conscious of unease and a difficulty in breathing.

This old tale of murder and evil is beginning to get to me. I have been immersed in reading the confusing accounts, and tracking down stray scraps of information for some time. I have studied the three murder hammers behind bullet-proof glass in the Cherryvale Museum. To this point, it has been simply a complex and fascinating story of long ago, with none of my emotions involved.

Suddenly — these four wicked people are coming alive to me.

Should I beware of rattling old bones? Am I disturbing painful rest? Tomorrow I set out on another search for information. We shall see if I am meant to continue.

Wednesday, May 8, 1991

I had planned to drive to Topeka to search the archives of the Kansas State Historical Society today, but I awakened to rain, and I take this as a portent that I should not go.

Thursday, May 9, 1991

The sun is shining; I have had an exciting conversation with a by-stander whose grandfather planted his feet firmly in the cemetery and announced, "This is where we buried them!", and the story has me hooked all over again.

———————

My intent is to write an account of the Bender

murders, in as straight-forward fashion as I can manage. I will choose the versions that I believe to be true, from the dozens of conflicting tales.

When I have re-told this story, according to my belief, then I shall chronicle the confusing and contradictory accounts that have been written, and list the sources.

My purpose is not to provide the final solution, for this is impossible. Too many pairs of eyes, too many family recollections, too many deathbed confessions, have muddied these murky waters.

In the one hundred eighteen years since the discovery of Dr. York's body in the apple orchard, there has not been a flagging of interest in this case. Every month brings a request for information. And so — let us begin.

It had been five years since Ulysses S. Grant and Robert E. Lee met in the Mclean house in Appomattox. There, on April 12, 1865, they signed the papers that ended the most violent and bloody of conflicts, the War Between the States. Hundreds of thousands of survivors began straggling back to their homes, ready to pick up their lives and make a fresh start.

In Kansas, this treaty signified the end of the border warfare which had dogged the attempts at settlement in the eastern part of the state, as Missouri Confederates sought to press their advantage over settlers in the fledgling Union state.

So far-reaching was the effect of this border warfare that Austin Thomas Dickerman, first county clerk of Labette County, wrote in 1878, "...all the

3

country south of that point (the Catholic Mission), was made perfectly desolate, not a vestige of anything like the improvements being allowed to remain. ...At that time (July, 1865) there was not a single resident on the land that is called Labette county...."

On September 29, 1865, the Osage Indian tribes, with Little White Hair as their head chief, signed a treaty with the Federal Government, at the Canville Trading Post, in which treaty the Osages agreed to re-locate. This, following the passage of the Homestead Act by Congress in May of 1862, allowing any person over the age of twenty-one, head of the family, and citizen of the United States, to settle on a piece of land, improve it, and after five years of residence, to own the land, gave an added inducement to settlement.

With the end of the War, settlers and homesteaders began swarming into the area, to claim their spots and begin their homesteads.

White families also streamed into Montgomery, Chautaqua, and other counties west, even though these were not part of ceded lands, and were set aside as the Osage Diminished Reserve.

A swindle against the Osages in the Diminished Reserve was attempted that same year. The Sturgess brothers of Chicago, with others, in the interest of Leavenworth, Lawrence, and Galveston Railroad Company, persuaded the Osages to sign a treaty for the sale of the entire diminished reserve for $100,000. Luckily, the "Sturgess Steal" was opposed in Congress and withdrawn.

Later that year, another swindle was attempted, as the Secretary of Interior deeded all the ceded lands to above mentioned railroad, and the Missouri, Kansas, and Texas Railroad Company. The Governor of Kansas successfully interceded for the settlers in this action.

Hundreds and thousands of squatters came into the area and staked out claims before the land had even been surveyed by the government.

By 1870, the white settlers' petitions to the government in Washington for a treaty to remove the Indians from this land, would result in the signing of the Drum Creek Treaty. This treaty provided for the Osages to give up 8,000,000 acres of Reserve Land in exchange for 78,000 acres on their reserve in Indian Territory. Under a large oak tree more than one hundred chiefs, sub-chiefs, and councilors affixed their signatures.

This being done, the land was officially open for settlement, and in March and April of 1871 the actual government surveys began.

This was "after the fact" in Labette County. Here, in 1866, a family came in an ox-drawn wagon, and settled on the banks of the creek named for the Osage Chief, Big Hill Joe.

The little girl, Alice, would tell on her 100th birthday, "There were only seven white families on the creek, and none on the prairies."

More families must have arrived steadily, for by 1868 a log school house had been built, and by 1869 another school, and a charter given for a Methodist Church.

This, then, was the setting for the arrival, one October day in 1870, of two men in a horse-drawn wagon. The wagon was a bit peculiar, having the rear wheels wider apart than the front.

They came driving over the old Osage Trail, which led from Ft. Scott through the Osage Mission, by Ft.

Roach at Ladore, down through the mounds to Cherryvale, and on to Independence. The long slough grass waved around them in gold and brown, the bright blue skies of October surrounded the senses, and the two travelers may as well have been traveling the Sahara.

The younger man was the driver. The older sat drawn into himself — giving no hint to the huge size and strength that were his. They reined in at the trading post of Rudolph Brockman and August Ern.

Not much of a thriving business. A few items to trade to the Indians who hadn't moved on after the Canville Treaty, but were encamped on Big Hill Creek. A few staples for the settlers — because Ft. Scott was the closest trading spot, and Parsons and Cherryvale were each just a sprinkling of houses.

So — crawling stiffly down from the wagon — and the younger responding, "I'm John Bender, and this is my pa, John Bender," and the older man muttering a greeting — Brockman recognized kindred spirits, and struck up a conversation in "low Dutch."

Apparently the German language was not the only thing they held in common, for later events would prove Rudolph Brockman to be fully as capable of evil as his new friends.

Young John was a strapping young man with a fair to ruddy complexion. He stopped short of being handsome because of his close-set eyes, and his mannerism of a nervous giggle.

The older man seemingly did not speak or understand English, except for a few cuss words. He would have stood over six feet in height, had it not been for his habitual stoop. He had broad, powerful arms, and a swarthy bearded face. Some neighbors later described him as "like a gorilla." One wouldn't

6

have wanted to meet him down a lonely road.

As young John talked about their plans to stake a claim for themselves, a deal was struck, and the strangers camped in their wagon close by the trading post that night.

Early next morning, Billy Toles was herding his cattle to open range, and saw Ern driving the two strangers around to look at available pieces of land.

Billy reported to his brother Silas that he guessed they would have new neighbors — because in a half-day's time the two men had staked out their claims.

They registered their claims at Humboldt, since there was no land office closer. Remember — the government was still swindling the Osages on the Diminished Reserve, and Independence had not yet been successful in becoming the site for the Land Office. Probably registering legally was not an over-riding concern, considering the common practice of pulling up stakes and adjusting boundaries to suit the settlers' convenience.

Pa Bender chose his 160 acres on the northeast corner of section 13, township 31, range 17. Rudolph Brockman's claim was the southeast corner of section 13.

For some strange reason, instead of choosing the usual rectangular 160 acres, young John plotted a strip of land a mile long and an eighth of a mile wide just north of his father's claim. Could it be that he was looking ahead to keeping neighbors from settling close by?

The elder Bender's choice was cunningly chosen for the business the two had in mind. Their inn would be built 100 yards off the trail, in a location perfectly situated to offer overnight lodging to those travelers going between Ft. Scott and Independence.

From this location, three dwellings were visible — the Toll brothers to the northeast three quarters of a mile, the Tyke cabin south a mile, and the Brockman-Ern trading post on the other side of the hill. Only the roofs of these buildings were visible, so the privacy would be complete.

Young John and his pa were pointed to a gap in the mounds to Father Dienst's log house, when they needed firewood while house building. No trees were on their claim — just gently rolling prairie — and no trees these hundred plus years since then. They did set out a few apple seedlings, but never were sprouts used to more deadly purpose.

Father Dienst directed the strangers to Mr. Hill's place, and they purchased a load of wood from him.

Drinking water would be fetched in a jug from the trading post, and the horses could be watered from a pool of water on John's claim. This pool was at the head of Spill-Out Creek.

The other settlers in the area seemed content to put up a crude log cabin, or at the most, a hasty frame building. The Bender men, however, bargained for a load of stone. Mr. Heironymus owned the mound claim. Today Highway 160 cuts a path through the mound, but at that time it was an unbroken ridge, thickly peppered with sandstone — some stones appearing in huge slabs. In their load was one large slab that was fully three inches thick and seven feet square.

While young John was off to Ft. Scott for a load of lumber to build the house, the older Bender was laying the foundation. He measured off dimensions of sixteen by twenty-four feet. Today this might be an adequate size for a dining-room, or master bedroom. For the Bender family this space would make living quarters, kitchen, bedroom for four adults, grocery store, and inn.

With the foundation marked, Pa Bender began digging a well, and was fairly underway on the job when young John returned after a four days' absence.

The two men completed digging the well and walled it with part of their purchased stone. There is no record whether they reached a good supply of water, but when the well figures later in the story, it has become unspeakably foul.

The next task in the builders' schedule was the excavation of the cellar. This was designed to be seven feet deep, with a floor area of seven foot square. The builders made a passageway in the northeast corner of the cellar — somewhat like a tunnel. Some neighbors later guessed that this had been used to maneuver the huge seven-foot-square slab into the cellar for the flooring — but there could have been another purpose in mind as well. There was a trap door built into the flooring of the room just above the cellar — and two outer doors to the cellar. These were always kept padlocked.

Now for the house itself, which was built with a nine foot ceiling. The front door, facing the north, opened onto the trail, which ran east and west in front of the house. Two windows flanked the door, and another door opened to the south.

The establishment was now complete, except for a stable and corral. These were built of a framework of stout poles, which were covered with a thatching of hay or heavy grass. This hay was purchased from a farmer in the Drum Creek bottoms.

Everything was in place and ready for the arrival of the womenfolk. Young John made a crude sign which he lettered "GROCRY", and nailed above the front door. A pleasant and inviting spot now awaited the weary traveler along the Osage Trail. Just as dusk fell, he would find a hot meal, feed for his horse, and a safe place to bed down for the night.

Chapter 2

Leroy Dick pulled a memory from his storehouse of recollections, and recalled Kate and her ma, always referred to by the community as Mrs. John Bender, arriving in December of 1870. He remembers Kate and young John attending the Christmas exercises in Harmony Grove school house.

Other accounts place Kate and Ma's arrival in early winter of 1871. This seems more likely, considering the wealth of activity the two men had to accomplish before sending for the women.

Regardless of the date, it is known that as soon as preparations were complete, John and Pa went to Ottawa where they wired the two women to meet them. From where did the women travel? No one thought to inquire into that aspect, when the family became the objects of state, national, and international attention.

While the men awaited the arrival of the women, they purchased some household supplies: a cook stove and heater, an eight-day clock, a small stock of groceries, and a coop of chickens. Although it isn't mentioned, the purchase of a kitchen or dining table must have been included, for in a photograph of the Bender Inn taken the day after the family disappeared, a man is shown sitting on an overturned dining-room table, outside the door of the inn.

E.B. White, an Independence gunsmith, told in later years that Drs. Masterman and Fugate, attendants at the scene of the crime, brought to him a leaf out of the Benders' table, which they had taken as a relic. He remembered that he made canes for each of them out of their walnut table-leaf. So — add a walnut table to the supplies in the wagon.

With the arrival of the womenfolk in Ottawa, the four of them were ready for the return to the homestead. It was winter on the trail by now. By the time they had traveled as far as Osage Mission, the town came as a welcome relief. Here, even with the dispersal of the Osages, was a bustling center, site of three mail routes, stagecoach lines, fur trading post, and home of Jesuit priests striving to do missionary work with the Indians and whites.

From the Mission, the trail was less thickly traveled, but fairly easy terrain. Only a few small creeks had to be forded, or crossed over. Lone horsemen passed them occasionally. The landscape was barren and the prairie grasses a dull brown. The Bender family was covering the same route that many of the victims would travel in the months to come.

Who knows what feelings were theirs as they reined in at that barren homestead? Certainly their feelings and emotions were different from those of ordinary folk, or they could never have stayed together through those later hideous acts.

The womenfolk added a few homey touches when

they arrived. They hung a wagon canvas across the room — creating a bedroom apart from the grocery and meal section. The walnut table was placed in front of the canvas, with one chair brushing against it.

Kate pulled down young John's crudely lettered sign, flipped over, and lettered neatly on the reverse side, "GROCERIES", and replaced it.

It may have been several days before the community knew that the women had arrived. Billy Toll would have no need to herd his cattle to pasture in winter. Brockman and Ern were both bachelors at that point. Mrs. Tykes was eager to have a woman to visit, but was busy managing her small children.

The first neighbors to make the acquaintance of the newcomers would spread their impressions.

"Mrs. John Bender seems to be about fifty years old. She's as unfriendly as she can be. She didn't even say hello to us. I guess she doesn't speak much English. She's heavy-set, and has a tallow-white face on her. We thought Mr. Bender was an ugly cuss, but she's no improvement."

About Kate.

"Now, Kate, she's a real good-looking young woman. Has a good figure — dark hair that has auburn in it when she gets in the sunlight. She talks enough to make up for the other three all put together. And she's a flirt — she was battin' her eyes at every man around — even managed to brush up against my man when she was scoopin' out sugar. I guess she's figurin' on being neighborly though. She asked about Sunday School, and I told her about Leroy Dick's singing school."

Young John and Kate rode down past Heironymus Ridge to Harmony Grove for Sunday School. Some folks thought John was a few bricks shy of a full load,

13

but that was probably because of his everlasting giggle. There was very little difference of opinion about Kate. Descriptions of her ranged from good-looking to voluptuous, stunning, beautiful. She made an immediate impact on the community.

The concept of inborn evil has captured the imagination of religious philosophers and students since Adam and Eve. Is it possible to be born without a conscience — a soul? With Ma Bender, one might look at the dour, dumpy person and speculate that life had turned her mean and bitter. But with beautiful Kate — how could this friendly, intelligent exterior mask so completely the cold, unfeeling center of this creation? There must have been manifestations of this evil, and there are written accounts of such, but the stories were put down to exaggeration and self-aggrandization.

The young people were accepted into the community. People just stayed away from Ma Bender. Three years later, when the family disappeared, no one had sought to learn her given name, and sixteen years later, when a warrant for the arrest of the four was issued, she was listed as Kate Bender, Sr.

Young Kate learned that a hotel had been erected in the newly incorporated town of Cherryvale. She traveled the six miles to town and secured a job as a waitress. Undoubtedly she was an excellent waitress. She was quick, intelligent, attractive, and seemed possessed of a magnetism that drew men to her.

How long Kate worked in the position is not known. The hotel may have lasted only a short while, until settlers had finished building their own accommodations.

The Thayer _Headlight_ of December 17, 1873,

would mention in local news, "In Cherryvale two hotels are running. They are the "Nigh House" and the "Cherryvale Hotel." They will give you a good square meal either place."

Kate's place of employment was always mentioned as the "Cherryvale Hotel."

Six weeks seems to have been about as long as Kate could stick with her employment. She had more pressing matters to attend to. Her sense of importance as a "spiritualist" or "clairvoyant" demanded some attention.

She spread the word that she could do healing, and had contact with the other world.

Perhaps as early as that first year the family "business" came into operation. Stories of missing men began circulating. Many of them were trailed to southeast Kansas, where the trail went cold.

Joe Sowers, an easterner, set out for Kansas in the fall of '69. A man names Jones mysteriously vanished some time later.

Leroy Dick sets May of '71 as the time two Drum Creek fisherman found the body of a man in a water hole. His head had been smashed and his throat cut from ear to ear. He was identified as the missing Mr. Jones.

Since the body was found on the Bradley claim, and the neighbors were already suspicious of Bradley, ugly rumors immediately began to be spread about this settler. People remembered that there were often strange visitors around his place. He could be a horse thief. Or could be in cahoots with some of the renegade Indians who made frequent forays into their earlier homelands.

Jones' body was claimed by his relatives. Since there were no clues, and no one in charge of an investigation, the mystery faded into the background, and simply added fuel to the negative feelings about Bradley. Time would prove him to be no more menacing than a spy agent for the railroad company, whose purpose was to locate settlers favorable to the railway.

With such an obvious suspect at hand, there was no reason to suspect two young people who attended Sunday School frequently, an older man who was often seen studying his German Bible, and an older woman who diligently minded her own business.

No one questioned the fact that there was very little farming going on within the boundaries of those two claims. Most of the settlers were hanging on by their toenails, and not many were living lives of ease.

Someone helped the murderers dispose of Jones's horse and saddle. Since many young men in the community were by this time smitten with Kate's beauty, it was possible any one of them could have served as an accomplice. Rudolph Brockman was obviously under Kate's spell. In two years time he would have progressed to the point of exchanging love letters, receiving a tin-type of his love, and setting a wedding date — which Kate shifted around to suit her moods.

The summer moved on, through Kansas heat. Young John broke the sod on a small patch and planted some corn.

Kate and Mrs. Bender went to the bedside of an ailing neighbor, and pronounced some mumbo-jumbo over her. When a Parsons doctor made his appearance, the two women left in a state of great indignation. The doctor remembered feeling uneasy by the wild glare in Kate's eyes. But, then, some people have flights of imagination, don't they.

A man who came upon the Inn (sometimes called the Tavern), one dark night, and peered through the window before knocking, told of seeing Kate and a dark-haired women dancing naked in the center of a group of people who were playing guitars and strange flutes. He crept away, frightened, without going in. But he probably had a mite too much to drink, don't you think?

Fall came on. Father Ponziglione, making his wide circuits to carry the word to the Indians who had been pushed down into Indian Territory, and to bring the sacraments to the whites in this new frontier, had been successful in leading the people to build a beautiful Catholic Church in Cherryvale. The Methodists there had erected a church to house the flock that had its beginnings under the oak trees in Timber Hill. Young John and Kate continued to attend services at Harmony Grove.

The vivacious young Sunday School maiden showed a different side of her nature on several occasions.

A woman in the neighborhood had been suffering from an ailment for some time. When the local doctor could not effect a cure, she sent for Kate, the healer and spiritualist. Kate promised a cure, but warned that it would be slow.

The woman, having no funds to pay her healer, put up her sidesaddle as collateral. When, after some time, the illness was not better, the woman went to the inn to discontinue the treatments and get back her saddle.

Kate assured her she was too impatient, that she should spend the night and the family would conduct a seance.

The seance seemed to consist of wild gibberish and

17

passing from hand to hand a bowie knife, a gun, and a stout club.

The woman became thoroughly alarmed, and made an excuse to go outside. Maybe for a call of nature. There is no mention of privy or outhouse in descriptions of the homestead, so guests and family probably had to make their own arrangements.

The woman, being frightened, hid in the tall prairie grass by the stable, to see what would happen. She saw the two men come out the back door, walk around the yard, then come into the stable.

When they entered the stable, she put the distance of a half-mile between her and the pursuers, until she was forced to drop down in exhaustion.

Presently two horsemen came riding across the prairie, riding well apart, and searching carefully.

The woman maintained complete silence, as the men crossed and recrossed the prairie, sometimes almost trampling her in her hiding place.

When at last they gave up the search, the woman hurriedly covered the remaining distance to the creek, which she crossed, and then dropped into the brush and timber. After a rest, she pushed on, and came to the house of Joe Newman. Here she blurted out her story and repeated over and over, "They meant to kill me. I know those men meant to kill me."

After Mrs. Newman had calmed her down, and given her some breakfast, the decision was made to go the George Major's home and tell the tale. Majors was a justice of the peace.

George and his wife listened to the woman's story and believed it. Mrs. Majors thought George and Joe should ride down and demand the sidesaddle.

The men knew that Kate could claim the

unachieved cure was due to lack of faith on the part of the patient. There was no law to enforce a refund in such a case.

The woman admitted through her tears that she had no money for court costs.

The matter was hushed up. Later repetition of the story never mentions the woman's name. No doubt she kept silent about the terrifying incident, in fear of deadly reprisal.

Another woman was to tell of Kate's frenzied outbursts. This woman, a stout character, given to tramping the prairies with her shotgun, was intrigued by Kate's spiritualistic powers.

She had been to see Kate on several occasions. On one particular visit, all was pleasant through the afternoon. As twilight came, the Benders drew pictures of men on the wall, and thrust knives into them. Kate told her that spirits often commanded her to kill. She lunged at one of the figures on the wall, then slunk toward the old woman whispering that the spirits commanded her to kill the old woman — now.

The old woman ran away in such a hurry that she left her wraps behind her. She never again visited Kate for advice. She spread her story around the countryside. Since she was known to be eccentric, the neighbors listened, then went about their work.

As if anyone could believe such stories about a good-looking young girl. Remember? She came to the Sunday School picnic at Leroy Dick's farm, and two or three young fellows asked to see her home.

Chapter 3

The year of 1871 slipped closer to '72. Frost touched the persimmons and made them sweet for the women to bake persimmon puddings, and slow-cooked persimmon butter. Hickory nuts were ripe along the creek bottoms, and wild grapes were ready for jam.

Disquieting tales of missing men circulated, but then, these were hard times. Of more importance was the skulduggery going on in Washington to keep settlers from getting fair and legal claims to their land. And the rough and ready tactics being employed by little towns to insure the county seat being placed in one location or another.

In February of '72 there was a terrible blizzard in southeast Kansas. The Thayer <u>Headlight</u> reported the tragedy of a woman losing her way while struggling to reach her children's school. She was found on the prairie frozen to death. Entire areas were isolated for a week. After the thaw, the bodies of two men were found on the prairie close to Oswego. There would have been no connection with the victim found earlier in Big Hill Creek, except for the method of murder; skulls crushed by a heavy blow — and throats cut from ear to ear.

Leroy Dick's wife would remember, a year later, that she had looked out her window, in the middle of the storm, and witnessed a team laboring through the snow. When it stopped, momentarily, to allow one of the drivers to fix something about the wagon, she recognized old John Bender. After puzzling about it with Leroy, they concluded the men must have lost their bearings in the blinding snow.

This must have been early in the "murder" business, before the burials in the orchard became commonplace.

Colonel Alexander York, lately a commander in the Union Army, but by that time a state Senator, made a trip to Washington, D.C., financed by civic leaders in Independence, in an attempt to persuade U.S. Senator Pomeroy to order the Federal Land Office moved from Humboldt to Independence. All of the land open for claims was in the area of Montgomery County and edge of Labette. Trips to Humboldt were expensive, lengthy, and often inconclusive.

When Senator York was successful (through use of discreet blackmail) in securing Pomeroy's affirmation, York was returned to Independence with accolades and jubilant celebration. Some people thought that, due to this defeat, a bitter political gang was out to get Senator York.

Kate was getting even more brazen about her business as a medium. By June of '72 she would have a poster made, advertising her services.

Prof. Miss Katie Bender

Can heal all sorts of Diseases;

Can cure Blindness, Fits, Deafness and all
   such diseases,

Also Deaf and Dumbness.

Residence, 14 miles east of Independence,
   on the road from Independence to Osage
   Mission
   one and one-half miles South East of
   Norahead Station.

June 18, 1872   Katie Bender

She must have had willing accomplices to post these, for one of the notices turned up in Chetopa, and this was quite a journey for Katie to make.

Many women at that time claimed to have healing powers. The use of midwives was common; medical emergencies often arose; and doctors were scarce.

Mrs. Tykes, or more correctly, Mrs. Thomas Tyack, considered herself a "magnetic" healer. She was pulled into Katie's spell, and in the summer of '72, went with her husband to the inn for a seance. This consisted mainly of "table talking", which required all the participants to sit around a table, hands flat on the board, little fingers touching to form a connected chain, and gabbling at the table itself, to procure answers.

In the 1930's, when this writer participated in such parlor games, the table often cooperated in an unexplained fashion. We knew nothing of the origin of this practice — could it have been a legacy of the evil Benders?

The first of the "circles" that the Tyacks attended produced no results, and Thomas rebelled at going again. Mrs. Tyack, however, went the second time.

Perhaps something scared her away, or perhaps the fee was too high, because she dropped the idea.

The "circles" were to exact a terrible price. After the disappearance of the Benders, when many innocent people were being harassed, Thomas, his wife, and daughter were arrested for complicity. Thomas and the daughter were released, but Mrs. Tyack was held for some time, and her daughter taken away from her care. The editor of the Headlight would protest the cruel treatment of a mother whose only crime came from visiting the fiendish Kate.

In the fall of '72, a bachelor named Johnny Boyle, living in Osage Mission, set out on foot going south one day, with $1,900 in his pocket. He planned to do some land buying. Although he apparently had no relatives to be concerned over his disappearance, he was listed among that ever-growing number of missing men.

On the 6th or 7th of November, Henry McKenzie, cousin to Leroy Dick's wife, came walking into the Dick's place one day. He had been living in Strawton, Indiana. Even though not a favorite relative, the Dick family gave him supper and he spent the night.

Henry had not settled down since the end of the War. His money went for flashy clothes, liquor, and women. On this occasion he was dressed to the nines with a wide Stetson, a showy cravat, stylish boots, and an expensive chinchilla coat.

He left the Dick residence the next morning to walk north for a visit with an Army buddy — J.H. Sperry. After a visit with his friend, Henry set out again on foot to visit his sister in Independence. In spite of his wealthy appearance, he had only 40 cents jingling in his pocket, and this loaned to him by his buddy.

Six miles would have put him in need of some refreshment, and he strode into the Bender place, ready to spend his 40 cents.

No one has any notion of the scenario from that point. Henry was young — 29 years old — had to be in good health, since he had just completed a trip on foot from Indiana. He managed to survive experiences in the War that would have finished off a lesser man.

One might argue that the Benders would have a difficult time murdering such an agile, wary victim. But Henry was afoot; carrying no weapon; from the looks of his clothing a wealthy man, and the strength of the Bender man was prodigious.

It must have been a shock to find this paltry sum on the dead man. Either rage over this fact — or, perhaps Henry's bawdy remarks to the duped Kate, must have incited the murderers, for Henry's body would be discovered terribly mutilated — with multiple stab wounds over his entire body. What else could incite such frenzy?

Ben Brown's money was not the cause of his death. He was thought to be carrying around $36 when he left his home in Cedar Vale, way over in Chautauqua County. What he did have was a fine, well matched team of sorrel horses and a new wagon and harness. After his disappearance, someone would spot one of those beautiful sorrels down in Indian Territory. When his body was found, naked except for a red and white silk handkerchief about his neck, he was still wearing a small silver ring on his little finger.

Kate was busy pursuing her hobby of spiritualism. Some uncharitable folk would later claim her to be a witch, or in the power of Satan. There would be descriptions of strange designs scratched in the floor of the house. These were said to be in the nature of 12 characters arranged around a three-foot circle. Seven columns of figures were found by these. Two little wooden figures, with nails driven into them, were found half-burned in the ash-heap.

A bit more definite is a verse copied in an old autograph book, dated 1873, and purchased from Kate for 50 cents:

Dullix, ix, ux,
You can't come over Pontio
Pontio is over Pilato!

This was to be recited in times of peril, while keeping the first two fingers of each hand crossed.

It might be argued that autograph verses were common, and had been handed down through generations. This is true, but most of these were flowery, or possessed of crude humor. There is something very different about Kate's verse. And Kate had no access to books or learning other than what she brought with her.

Some travelers were luckier than others. They could have been more on guard — they could have appeared at a propitious time — when a recent kill would have demanded some privacy.

A William Pickering told a tale so well believed that it was retold by many of the chroniclers of that day.

Mr. Pickering stopped to take a meal at the Inn. He was from back East, and finely dressed. He preferred to have toast rather than the heavy cornbread he was offered. Not only that, but he chose to sit on Pa's bench facing the canvas partition, rather than to sit with his back to the cloth, where he perceived several greasy spots or stains about the height of a man's head.

Kate turned abusive, and he shouted back at her that if he couldn't sit in the one clean spot, he wouldn't eat there at all. She came at him with a knife, and he simply hurried out, mounted his horse, and left. In his version, he was not frightened — merely disgusted.

A credible story, doubted by few, was told by Father Paul Ponziglione, the same priest mentioned earlier, who rode all over southeast Kansas and into Indian Territory. Father Paul had confronted dangers and difficulties of all dimensions, and was not given to exaggeration.

In this instance, construction of the large Catholic Church in Osage Mission (present-day St. Paul), was underway, and Father Paul was collecting generous sums of money for the projects.

Father Paul reined in at the Tavern, thinking to spend the night. He was well acquainted with the disappearances happening in southeast Kansas, and undoubtedly on edge. He told of seeing Pa place a hammer on the other side of the canvas partition, then watching uneasily as Kate and Pa carried on a low conversation. Becoming more and more alarmed, he made the excuse of need to tend his horse. He mounted up and galloped away, and always thereafter credited a higher Power for saving his life. So well-known and respected was Father Paul, that a higher Power may, indeed, have stayed the murderer's hands.

Not so fortunate was Bill McCrotty, who lived near Osage Mission. His family saw him leave home with nearly $2,600 in his pocket. As his body, clad only in underwear, lay out on the prairie to be claimed, identification would be simple because of a tatoo on his left arm in Indian ink:

W.F. McCrotty, Born 1843

and under it, drawn an American flag.

Who knows about John Greary? One source lists his name as those identified at the exhumation, but this source omits the name of Johnny Boyle. Another source credits Greary with carrying $2,000 when he disappeared. How Greary's name enters the list is uncertain, since none of those directly involved ever list his name.

Now we come to the point in the affair where the greed and cold-hearted brutality of the killers would prove their undoing.

George Loncher, his wife and little daughter were settling on a claim south of Independence. The young wife contracted a fatal illness and was laid to rest in Fawn Creek Cemetery. The grief-stricken father, knowing he was unable to care for his little girl and wrest a living from the soil at the same time, determined to take the child to her grandparents in Iowa, where she would be cared for until he was able to send for her. He bargained with a nearby doctor, William York, for a team and wagon.

The father and child set out, and were known to have stopped overnight in Coffeyville, where a sympathetic woman would dress the child on the following morning in new clothes which the woman provided.

The two never reached the home of the anxious grandparents. Word came back to the doctor and home community that the father and child had vanished somewhere on the trail.

Fear gripped the area. Many were in terror that the fiend which roamed southeast Kansas had snatched two more victims. Had they known — the truth was more horrible than any imagined ghoul roaming their prairies and valley.

Dr. York was deeply concerned about the missing father and daughter. He began immediate inquiries and planned searching parties.

He was not aware of a discovery in the woods near Ft. Scott, when he started out from his Independence home to drive to Ft. Scott on business.

Having completed his business, he somehow heard of the discovery. A few days earlier a wagon team had been found abandoned in the woods near Ft. Scott. The horses were nearly starved. Some clothing was found in the wagon belonging to a man and some to a little girl. No clue to the man and girl could be found.

Dr. York at once went to view the wagon and team, and positively identified them as the same he had sold a few days earlier to George Loncher.

The March 28 Lawrence Tribune would state: "He returned to Ft. Scott, attended to his business, and on Sunday left for home. Since that time nothing has been seen or heard from him."

Without a doubt, Dr. York must have seen incriminating evidence, when he spent the night at the Bender Inn. He would have made a tempting target in himself — well dressed, riding a red roan pacing mare, and thought to have been carrying between $700 and $900 in his money belt. But the Benders were cautious about choosing well-known local victims — there had been an unprecedented search for the missing father and daughter — and the net seemed to be tightening about them.

Would avarice and greed have gotten the better of their judgement? Or would the doctor have confronted them in such a positive way that he sealed his own doom?

He never returned to his home on Fawn Creek, or to his ailing wife. This time, however, the Benders had gone too far. There was among the doctor's survivors, his brother, Colonel Alexander York, who had been known among the men who served under him as cold and hard a leader as could be. None ever chose to cross him of their own free will.

The wife of the missing doctor reported her fears to her brother-in-law. That was the beginning of the end of the Benders.

Chapter 4

—◄—●—►—

Col. York lost no time. With his brother Ed, he went to Ft. Scott and began a painstaking retracing of William's return journey.

Their first clue was from Mr. J.C. White, who lived 12 miles from Ft. Scott, on the Osage Mission road. Mr. White confirmed that Dr. York had fed and watered his horses at White's residence.

From there they found another clue at the home of Mr. Harvey Burns. The doctor had inquired the time of day there, and the distance to Osage Mission.

More detective work would reveal that a clerk in Parsons had sold cigars to a man answering the description of Dr. York. Someone would recall the doctor saying he planned to spend the night at the Bender Inn.

Now the York brothers would zero in on the Big Hill area.

With 12 helpers, chiefly from the Cherryvale vicinity, they began to search the streams and waterholes around the trail.

They rode in to the Bender's place and continued

their investigation. Kate was most helpful, and offered to do a seance, or to consult her charts. The Colonel was not impressed with her credentials, and did not promise to return for her advice.

Young John produced a decoy story — telling how he had been waylaid and shot at on one occasion. He led the party to a tree which he claimed to have been the ambush spot. The Colonel and his party gave no credence to his story, and rode away feeling they had wasted their time.

The search party continued, exploring along the Verdigris River for any trace of the missing doctor.

The time for the annual school election came around. For many years it was tradition, or probably law, that the second Tuesday in April was set for election of the local school board. Teachers were expected to either supervise their charges away from the building for the afternoon — or school would be dismissed. This election was considered a sacred obligation to the community members — for the school was the center of the rural neighborhood — and self-governance was an important power.

There was a larger attendance than usual at Harmony Grove that April of 1873. Young John was there, and Pa, who was his customary taciturn self.

The school election was taken care of in record time, and the talk turned to the terrible disappearances that had by now led to their very own community.

"What we need to do," someone said, "is to search every foot of each of our farms."

"You're welcome to start your search on my place," offered Father Dienst.

Other offers followed in short order, and participants got more and more vocal about the kind of punishment that should be dealt to the criminals.

Young John and Pa apparently lost interest, and drifted away from the meeting.

The group made plans for a mass meeting to be held at the schoolhouse on April 12, for the purpose of forming a plan of action. Each was asked to spread the word to all who were interested. The school election was on April 8, so this would give four days to communicate the plan.

Buried in the back pages of the Thayer <u>Headlight</u> in the next day or two, along with advertisements for the celebrated Mitchell Wagon — the Cayuga Chief — was an article describing the finding of an abandoned team and wagon, with a little Scottish terrier apparently guarding it, in the woods outside of Thayer.

No one took any notice of this news item down around Big Hill way. There were too many other matters demanding attention.

Col. York came back in a couple of days to the Bender place, with as many as 50 men in the search party. He planned to question Kate still further. There seemed to be no one home at the Bender's so the party continued their hunt elsewhere.

The mass meeting called for April 12 brought out a large number of men — about 75. The small schoolhouse would have been bulging at the seams. Apparently this was business for men only — no mention was made of women or children attending.

The tone was grim. The time had come for action, and the men intended to initiate some. The Thayer <u>Headlight</u> editor had his own priorities. The article would not appear until the April 29 issue.

April 29, 1873
At a meeting of the citizens of Osage Township,

Labette County, Kansas, held at the schoolhouse in District #30, April 12, 1873.

W.A. Starr was called to the chair, D.D. Lindsay appointed Secretary and the following preamble and resolutions were unanimously adopted.

Whereas, Several persons from adjoining counties are missing, and supposed to have been murdered; and,

Whereas, Suspicion appears to rest upon the citizens of this community, and believing ourselves to be unjustly accused, therefore

Resolved, That a committee be appointed, and report at our next meeting,

Resolved, That we heartily sympathize with the friends of those who have been slain, and that the citizens of Osage Township, will make every effort in our power to detect and bring to justice the murderers,

Resolved, That the Independence, Parsons, Chetopa, Thayer, and Osage Mission newspapers be requested to publish the foregoing resolutions.

Prior to the printing of the resolutions, in fact, just four days after the mass meeting, the editor devoted several columns to Thayer's own private mystery. This was important enough to edge forward from the back pages, and closer to the world news, which occupied the entire front page.

April 16, 1873

There is no longer any doubt in the minds of our people that a dreadful crime of some nature has been perpetrated. Henry Hostetter of SW Coal Company, says he saw a man at the wagon three times on the day before the horses were brought up to town in his shirt sleeves and several others saw a man there with his coat on.

Mr. Otis Richmond says he saw the dog, that was found guarding the team, trying to get on the car Saturday morning and that it ran after the train after it started. This would indicate that the owner of the dog took the cars here. A few days ago we went down to Wheeler's stable and the faithful dog was still with the wagon and barked furiously when we went near it. On the bottom of the wagon we saw a piece of flooring board nailed over a hole on which was daubed in crude letter "GROCRY". Pulling this off we found on the other side the same style — "GROCERIES".

The wagon has been considerably worn, the hind wheels are both dished the wrong way by being too heavily loaded and two of the spokes of the right hind wheel are broken. The horse and mare found with the team are both lame. The yearling colt is in good order. They are still in the possession of A.H. Wheeler. It is now 11 days since they were found, and no light has been thrown on the mystery yet. Last Monday week, the wagon was brought up from the ravine near town and in it was found a double barreled shotgun. One barrel was loaded and the other empty. The one that was loaded had a charge of buckshot on top of an ordinary load of common shot. The side of the wagon box was full of shot.

We hope papers throughout the country will call attention to this.

From the Tuesday, April 29, printing of the resolution, almost a week would elapse before the Sunday afternoon singing school at Harmony Grove. This was led by Leroy Dick.

Billy Toll drove his cattle past the Bender Inn, on his way to Sunday School, and was struck by the deserted appearance of the place.

As he drove the herd back, after Sunday School, he was struck again by the empty look of the place, and stopped to investigate The peculiar actions of a sow in a pig sty caught his attention. The mother pig would stagger drunkenly and squeal in a piteous way.

He rounded the corner of the house, and reeled from the stench coming from the stable. When he freed the sow, she plunged down the draw and buried her snout in the cool water. She was so famished from lack of water that Billy had to drive her back to the pen, lest she founder.

Covering his nose, he advanced on the stable. He became hot with indignation when he discovered the source of the revolting smell. A young calf had been tied to a post, had died of starvation, and was badly decomposed. The mother of the calf had been unable to reach her baby, and her udders had burst. These sights reminded Billy that loose Bender stock had been wandering around his place for days.

He circled the house and found a broken window pane. Pushing a stick through the opening, he thrust aside the blind and saw a silent, empty house.

As he rounded up his herd, he was so excited by this mystery that he stopped the first travelers he met, and blurted out the story to them.

The travelers were Schwartz and Brooks, partners in a real estate firm, who were showing a load of prospective settlers from the east.

They were intrigued by the mystery, and announced their intention to stop and take a look.

Billy herded his cattle into the corral and told his

brother Silas the news. Then he galloped back down the road to have another look.

The real estate party were milling around and discussing, with liberal bursts of profanity, the kind of people who would cause such suffering of animals. They announced that the team had gotten loose, or had disappeared. This led Billy to the discovery that the wagon was also missing.

With the certainty that the house was deserted, the men broke the lock and entered the building.

Things looked strewn about, but in no particular way to incite suspicion. Billy had seen it plenty of times, and it looked about as always.

Here was some exciting news to spread to the community. If he hurried, Billy could make it back down to Harmony Grove before singing school was over.

The crowd was just coming out the door as Billy galloped in. Leroy Dick was still inside, putting away the songbooks, and setting things in order.

The stir created by his news was all that Billy's heart desired. Men and woman alike were riled up over the mistreatment of the animals. Leroy Dick would know nothing of the story until he and his wife reached home.

Leroy, feeling his responsibility as a township trustee, rode back to the schoolhouse that night to find out particulars.

Billy repeated his story, and told about the Schwartz and Brooks party breaking into the house.

Leroy objected to the action, saying this should not have been done without having an officer present. He promised to ride over the next day and make some disposal of the remaining stock. Many of the men there agreed to meet him at that time.

As Leroy rode to the Bender place, early Monday morning, he was mentally cataloging the number of stock he would be looking for. It hadn't been too many months since he had been taking inventory of the animals, as part of his duty as township assessor.

Leroy and Mrs. Bender had argued over the numbers; he insisting he counted 18 head of cattle; she protesting that the number varied since Young John often traded and sold. If the number of horses passing through their hands had been included, there would certainly have been a sharp variance.

The remains of the corn crop that young John had raised in '72 were still in the crib, but no crops had been raised on Pa's homestead. Young apple sprouts were growing, hit or miss, as if someone had thrown out seeds and paring. The neighbors marveled at the cultivation given to that small patch of apple sprouts.

As Leroy tied his horse to the corncrib, he caught a whiff of a vile odor. The horrors of the Civil War were too fresh in his mind to cause any doubts about the stench. Somewhere there was a body decomposing.

By virtue of his township position, Leroy had the authority to break the lock and enter the house. He first broke the padlock and opened the cellar. He found it to be empty, with the dirt walls crumbled, packing the crevices around the huge stone slab.

The interior of the house was as crude and unfinished as the day it was built. No lathes, plastering, or covering of any kind was on the walls or ceiling. A lid which fitted into an opening in the kitchen floor could be lifted with a boot-strap nailed to one end, and this formed an entrance to the cellar. This would become, in lurid accounts of the tragedy, the celebrated "trap door", "hidden trap door", "concealed entrance", "pathway to the pit of horrors."

Among contents left strewn in the house were three hammers of varying sizes, an eight-day clock with an inner compartment found to contain some pieces of jewelry, a combination meat saw and knife, and a German Bible.

Leroy's first concern was to make arrangements for the care of the stock. George Mortimer agreed to put the cattle with his herd. Moneyhon agreed to take care of the chickens and ducks.

With this done, Leroy rode around the neighborhood asking for help on the following day. He asked men to bring teams, plows, and shovels. Of the men who were contacted and agreed to help were: Douglass, Hornback, McCrumb, Ben Ferguson, Maurice Sparks, George Mortimer, and Mr. Coleman. Leroy also sent word to Col. York.

After making his rounds, he met Ferguson and Sparks again. They were in a state of agitation. Someone had finally caught sight of the article in the <u>Headlight</u>, and the coincidence was overpowering.

Leroy Dick needed to be present at the Bender place the following morning to direct the search, so the decision was made that Ferguson and Sparks should go to Thayer to identify the team and wagon.

There was, of course, no question, and the two were able to make a positive identification.

The following morning men converged at the Bender Inn, and the grim task was set to begin.

Chapter 5

On Tuesday morning George Mortimer brought his plow, as requested. Other men brought spades and shovels. Leroy brought his wagon rod to use as a probe.

Leroy Dick's brother, Temple, took a group of men to check out the waters of Spill-Out Creek, whose branches twisted and turned for three miles before converging on young John's claim.

David Lindsey took another group to check the stable and corral.

Leroy's group started digging the dirt-packed crevices around the huge cellar slab — thinking to pry it up for investigation. Suddenly Si Toll's spade sank deeper than usual — into soft, vile muck. Such an overpowering stench flowed from this opening that the men came tumbling out of the cellar in various stages of nausea.

At this point in the search, the men still expected to find bodies under the stone slab, and felt there must be some way of removing the floor. Leroy took a heavy sledge hammer and managed to break some chunks from the stone.

On one of his trips up for air, he became aware of the crowd approaching. Men were coming from all directions — on foot, in oxcarts, wagons, buckboards, on horseback — long straggling lines over every trail. About forty men had started the search — by mid-afternoon it was estimated there were a thousand.

One team and buggy were seen approaching from the Brockman place. This vehicle was overtaking and passing all slower conveyances.

When the team reached the crowd, Edward York and Henry Beers sprang out of the buggy. Ed explained that his brother, Sen. York, was busy with court duties and could not help, but that Ed and Mr. Beers were qualified to make identification, if need arose.

Leroy gave the two a run-down on findings to that point — futile search of Spill-Out Creek, lack of results around stable and corral, the nauseating stench from the cellar keeping down further discovery there.

The pressure from the milling crowd threw the scene into confusion. Suggested plans rang out from all directions. Leroy was so agitated, and in such a state of nerves from his noxious task, that when he spun his story in chronological fashion, at the age of 90, he would not recall or mention the next action in the search.

Certain it is, from many accounts, that several of the men found some long poles, or rails, pried under the corner of the house, and succeeded in moving it over so that the cellar lay exposed. Evidence of this is seen in a photo of the house, taken a few days later, with a long pole still wedged under one corner of the house.

This method of moving the house was commonly used in that era. The writer's own grandfather employed this method, in the early 1900s, to move his dwelling from one location to another which was more to his liking.

The men who moved the house found the cellar empty, with the blood that caused the stench coming from the soaked dirt around the edges of the slab, rather than from any bodies under the flooring.

A newspaper account of the cellar with its "loose pavement of stones" would correspond with Leroy's account of breaking pieces off the huge slab with the sledge hammer. This, of course, he did before the crowd assembled.

Memory is selective, and often plays us false. With the confusion and excitement, remarks picked up from bystanders and eyewitnesses found their way into newspaper accounts. These were printed as actual proof, and served to perpetuate many myths that accumulated.

The editor of a local paper, who heard various people talk about Dr. York's brother helping to give directions, jumped to the conclusion that it was Col. York being mentioned, rather than Ed York, and printed the news that way. A later fiction writer would use this newspaper story as a basis to discredit the major portion of Dick's account.

With the frustration of an empty cellar, and the uncertainty of what the next step should be, there was a mounting sense of rage and impotence. Dr. Keebles of Thayer pronounced the bloodstains on the stone slab and around the opening to the cellar to be human blood. Ed York found a piece of bridle in the house and knew it was from his brother's rig. More ominous was the discovery of Dr. York's glasses —

silver-rimmed with a broken piece in the frame patched together with solder. Ed remembered that his brother had been blind as a bat while the glasses were being repaired.

Action was so nearly at a standstill that Ed York got back in the buggy and sat dejectedly, wondering what course of action to undertake next. He let his gaze wander over the bleak surroundings. Something unexpected caught his sight. Seated as he was, above the heads of the crowd, facing against the afternoon sun, he caught a rectangular depression in the ground by the young apple trees. This ground had been kept well cultivated by the Benders. In the two weeks since their disappearance, the ground had hardened, and was now showing deep cracks in the shape of a rectangle.

Ed was electrified. "Boys," he yelled, "I see a grave!"

Several young men scrambled to the ridgepole of the house and called down that they, too, could see the depression, and several others nearby.

Now the workers were galvanized into action. They seized probes, spades, and shovels, and started digging. In Leroy Dick's mind he would see his being the shovel to make first contact with the body. Others would make the same personal claim.

When the nearly nude body was unearthed — face downward, base of skull smashed, legs bent upward, turning it over disclosed the throat cut completely around. Ed York and Henry Beers made instant identification. The two pulled back in horror and retreated to the sidelines.

Leroy felt helpless about the necessary procedure. He had been elected to his township position with no training and no experience.

With the state of decomposition and the gaping wound, he and Dr. Keebles feared that removing the body and sudden exposure to air might preclude positive identification.

They discussed in low tones what could be done. Dr. Keebles made a tentative proposal that — if a strong-stomached volunteer could be found — and providing Ed York gave his approval — the head might be completely severed from the body, and made available for identification.

This brother Ed agreed to, and Leroy, himself, completed the decapitation. With the head severed, washed, and hair parted, Ed and Henry made the identification and set off at once for Independence for securing a coffin, and returning for the body.

By this time, it was too late to continue digging. Leroy was troubled about the legal ramifications. The nearest coroner was thirty miles away. Leroy knew that the Colonel, when he arrived, would overstep the law, and claim possession and removal of the body at once.

In the midst of this problem, Tom Mortimer pointed out that a constable and justice of the peace had the authority of this release.

Ed Newman and George Majors, both in the crowd there, served in those capacities. They were summoned, joined with Leroy in measuring the fractures in the skull — which matched exactly the little hammers found in the kitchen, and rendered their verdict. This allowed the release of the body.

Colonel York and Ed arrived around midnight, with a coffin for their brother's body, and removed it for burial.

The few remaining searchers returned to their homes for a short interval of troubled sleep.

Early next morning when Leroy and the other neighbors met for their gruesome work, they would be dumbfounded at the size of the crowd already gathered. Word had traveled with lightning speed. By afternoon the estimate would be between two and three thousand.

Given a crowd of this size, and the highly emotional state of the search party, it is not surprising that many contradictory stories should emerge.

The men had thought to start plowing Hell's Half Acre, but a preliminary probe with the rod, in the vicinity of the doctor's grave, led to another discovery.

Shovels were busy, and there came to light the body of Henry McKenzie. Leroy was incredulous. He and his wife hadn't guessed that cousin Henry was missing. In view of his disappearances and past erratic behavior, no one had given a thought when he failed to show at his sister's house in Independence. His sister had not even known to expect him.

The noisy crowd fell silent before this horror, then talk burst out.

"Who'd they say it was?"

"You say Mr. Dick didn't even know his cousin was missing?"

"You suppose there's another body?"

The next probing, and the subsequent digging, would lead to the body of W.F. McCrotty, with his head badly smashed.

Again the crowd stilled — the identification made — again the crescendo of outbursts. The workers were beginning to tire. The human mind can absorb just so much horror. Surely this little patch of swaying apple seedlings held no more terrible secrets.

The next probe and digging revealed the body of a small man, horribly mutilated, obviously the subject of barbarous cruelty.

None of the search party and none in the crowd could identify the man. His nude body lay exposed to the world, while the searchers moved to the next discovery.

More parallel tracks in the plowed soil — another yield to the probe.

This time the grave gave up the body of Benjamin Brown of Cedar Vale — he of the finely matched sorrel team — with the little silver ring on his finger. Was he known to someone there? Or how was identification so certain that Mrs. Brown would arrive soon to make arrangements for shipping his body for burial.

But there was more grim work to be done. Another cluster of parallel tracks appeared. This unearthing would send the crowd into a hysterical, frenzied mob. For here was found the body of George Loncher, with his little girl, a silk scarf knotted tightly around her neck, dumped into the grave with him. The doctor, making an examination of the bodies, told the men nearby that the child had been buried alive.

The news spread in shock waves throughout the crowd. Tears streamed down cheeks, imprecations were hurled through the air — this latest horror seemed more than could be borne.

One could stiffen the spine and close the mind to the hideous outrages against the murdered men — but a little girl? None could imagine anyone in human form taking part in burying alive an innocent child. As Ivan Karamazov put the question of evil, "What have children to do with it, tell me, please?"

But the afternoon wore on, and the ground might have other tales to be told.

There seemed to be no more parallel cracks. There <u>was</u> a sort of round depression near the graves. Again spades and shovels were employed. The tools cut into a filled-in well. Here, at a depth of seven feet, was found the body of Johnny Boyle — in a sitting position. Johnny — who went his own way — taking no advice from anyone.

At this point Leroy may have taken a temporary reprieve — or have gone to see about pine boxes for cousin Henry and the unidentified man.

Other accounts would list John Greary's name in the list of bodies. Leroy never made mention of his name, and the photograph made later, with all graves notated, and coffins waiting nearby, made no mention.

The editor of the <u>Headlight</u>, who was late in getting to the day's unfolding tragedy, recorded in his paper — "...Five of the bodies were still lying on the ground, and were almost entirely naked."

He listed Brown, McCrotty, unidentified man, McKenzie, and Loncher and little girl.

One other source tells of finding the body of a young woman, so terribly mutilated that it was difficult to tell her sex for some time. The same source claims that, in one common grave, were found the dismembered limbs of several bodies, some of which had been partially burned.

In the above mentioned source is the only tale of a newlywed couple who stopped at the Inn. The young groom was killed, then the young bride was raped by both young John and Pa, before being killed in her turn.

Most accounts list the number of bodies found there to be eight. At least two accounts put the number at eleven.

Many facets of the Bender murders would keep this horror alive in the minds of people across the nation — the complete callousness of the criminals — the burying alive of the child — the length of time the secrets were kept — the lack of suspicion until the very end — the intrusion of the occult and sense of another world of evil. No aspect was more terrifying than the setting — a beautiful, serene corner of the prairie, with softly rounded hills, wavy grasses, and meadowlarks singing along the roadway. Surely darkness and death had no place there.

Kate's handbill, posted throughout the area. (Kansas Historical Society, Topeka, Kansas)

GOVERNOR'S PROCLAMATION.

$2,000 REWARD

State of Kansas, Executive Department.

WHEREAS, several atrocious murders have been recently committed in Labette County, Kansas, under circumstances which fasten, beyond doubt, the commissions of these crimes upon a family known as the "Bender family," consisting of

JOHN BENDER, about 60 years of age, five feet eight or nine inches in height, German, speaks but little English, dark complexion, no whiskers, and sparely built;

MRS. BENDER, about 50 years of age, rather heavy set, blue eyes, brown hair, German, speaks broken English;

JOHN BENDER, Jr., alias John Gebardt, five feet eight or nine inches in height, slightly built, gray eyes with brownish tint, brown hair, light moustache, no whiskers, about 27 years of age, speaks English with German accent;

KATE BENDER, about 24 years of age, dark hair and eyes, good looking, well formed, rather bold in appearance, fluent talker, speaks good English with very little German accent:

AND WHEREAS, said persons are at large and fugitives from justice, now therefore, I, Thomas A. Osborn, Governor of the State of Kansas, in pursuance of law, do hereby offer a **REWARD OF FIVE HUNDRED DOLLARS** for the apprehension and delivery to the Sheriff of Labette County, Kansas, of each of the persons above named.

In Testimony Whereof, I have hereunto subscribed my name, and caused the Great Seal of the State to be affixed.

[L. S.]   Done at Topeka, this 17th day of May, 1873.

THOMAS A. OSBORN,
Governor.

By the Governor:

W. H. SMALLWOOD,
Secretary of State.

Governor's Proclamation issued as a reward for capture. (Kansas State Historical Society, Topeka, Kansas)

51

The Bender house, taken the day of the grave digging. (Cherryvale Museum)

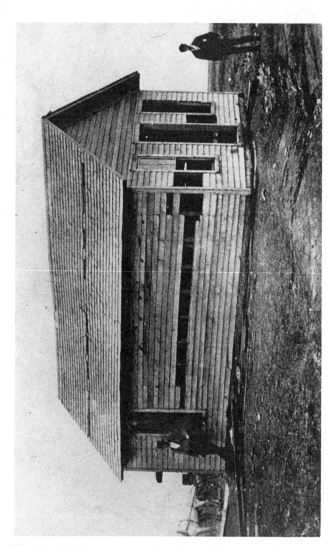

The Bender house, taken the day of the grave digging.
(Photographed by G.R. Gamble, Parsons, Kansas)

The Bender grave sites. (Photographed by G.R. Gamble, Parsons, Kansas)

THE BENDER SHANTY.—[From a Photograph by George R. Gamble.]

SCENE OF THE BENDER MURDERS.—[From a Sketch by John W. Howard.]

THE GRAVE OF DR. YORK.—[From a Photograph by George R. Gamble.]

THE BENDER MURDERS NEAR CHERRYVALE, KANSAS.—[See Page 480.]

Illustrations from <u>Harper's Weekly</u>, June 7, 1873.

The Bender Hammers; The Cherryvale Museum.
(Photographed by Brett Coomer)

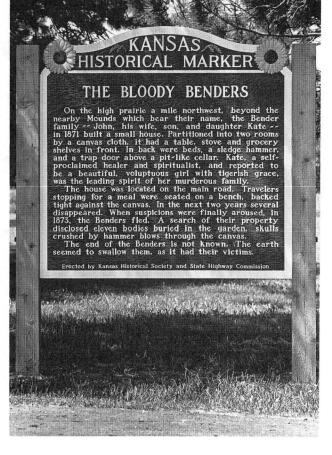

Historical Marker on U.S. Highway 160.
(Photographed by Brett Coomer)

Location of Bender Claim

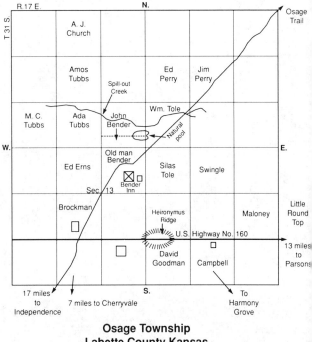

20 Miles to St. Paul

R.17 E. N.

T 31 S

Osage Trail

A. J. Church

Amos Tubbs

Ed Perry

Jim Perry

Spill-out Creek

M. C. Tubbs

Ada Tubbs

John Bender

Wm. Tole

Natural pool

W.

E.

Old man Bender

Ed Erns

Silas Tole

Swingle

Sec. 13

Bender Inn

Brockman

Heironymus Ridge

Maloney

Little Round Top

U.S. Highway No. 160

13 miles to Parsons

David Goodman

Campbell

17 miles to Independence

S.

7 miles to Cherryvale

To Harmony Grove

Osage Township
Labette County Kansas
1873

Chapter 6

---◄◄●►►---

With discovery of the bodies, the nightmare had just begun.

When Johnny Boyle's body was found in the well, and no more cracks appeared in the soil, the crowd needed an immediate vent for its anger.

Even though there were many solid, God-fearing Germans in the neighborhood and some in the search party itself — there were rumblings about the "low Dutch." Talk spread that someone in the area must have been an accomplice — that someone had alerted the Benders, and helped them escape.

Rudolph Brockman was known to have been a suitor of Kate's. He was not well-liked; several accounts circulated about him mistreating animals.

It was Brockman's misfortune to be present in the crowd when a culprit was needed. Several men began shouting at him to tell what he knew about the Benders. Such menace directed at him made Brockman nervous — so that he sputtered answers in German.

This was enough to ignite the powder-keg; a rope

was procured, tied around Rudolph's neck, and he was hauled up into the air. He was held there a bit, released, and he protested his innocence. This action was repeated, until even the most bloodthirsty had to admit nothing was being gained. He was described almost universally as "old Brockman" although a study of his headstone at Harmony Grove Cemetery proves that he was the ripe old age of 31 at the time.

Leroy Dick and his helpers came out, with the three murder hammers in Leroy's hands, and the attention of the crowd shifted immediately. Brockman made a quick getaway.

Before the day's activities closed, Mrs. Brown and McCrotty's people came to claim their loved ones, and relatives of the others must be notified. Leroy took charge of cousin Henry and the unidentified man, and the remaining bodies were given protection.

The next few days were occupied with burials and notifications, but the activity swirled around the patch of prairie like a malevolent wind.

A story came out in the Leavenworth <u>Times</u>:

> The Cherryvale excitement is still at fever heat. The <u>Times</u> has specials from that place tonight which give the following additional particulars: A force of about 100 men are at the grounds of the slaughter, which is being plowed over again, though no more graves have been found. The Roach family of Ladore, seven miles from the slaughter den, consisting of the old man and wife, son and wife and stepson John Haines and wife and Thomas Tyak, wife and daughter, have been arrested. A.M. King, a traveling district preacher, has been arrested at Parsons, and a

notorious murderer, once pardoned from the penitentiary, named Major Macford, and a woman with him, were arrested at Fort Scott. Detectives are still out, but the rumors are so contradictory that no reliance is to be placed in reports from them. The Bender house and furniture is being demolished by the visitors, who are carrying away portions of it as relics.

The mention of the souvenir hunters was accurate. With no one to restrain them, every visitor went away with a board from the house, a loose shingle, or even a stone from the well.

The Thayer <u>Headlight</u> ran the observation the following week: "...Thousands of people daily visit the grounds. Last Sunday it was estimated there were 3,000 people on the grounds at one time."

Jim Snoddy, a Ft. Scott marshall, Col. C.J. Peckham, and Henry Beers traveled to Thayer to check train departures at the time of the discovery of the abandoned team and wagon. The ticket agent told them that four people answering exactly the description of the Benders came in that night. They had funny looking baggage, including a doghide hair trunk, and things tied up in a white bedspread.

They wanted tickets on the earliest train to Humboldt, which was due at that very time. The old man did his talking in Dutch, which caused so much misunderstanding that he didn't even have time to count his change from a ten-dollar bill, before boarding the train. The ticket agent and some loungers watched them kick a little white dog off the train.

The Leavenworth, Lawrence, and Galveston Railway came south only as far as Thayer at that point in history. By going north to Humboldt, it was possible to switch to the MKT road and go south to Vinita, in Indian Territory, and from there on to Denison, Texas. Or one could continue north to Kansas City and there connect with trains to the East.

The <u>Tribune</u> of Independence ran an interview in the July 29, 1908, issue. This article quoted Captain James B. Ransom of Kansas City.

> I was a passenger conductor on the Leavenworth, Lawrence, Galveston now the Southern Kansas. I had charge of the train the night the Benders disappeared. Two men and two women, Germans, speaking broken English, boarded my train at Thayer, about eleven miles from the Bender home. They had tickets to Humboldt, but after we had left Humboldt, they were still on the train, and paid their fare to Kansas City. We reached here at 5 o'clock, in time to connect with trains for the East. When the search began for the Benders, who were Germans, I remembered my four passengers and told the detectives about them. While the posse were racing (sic) about the country the Benders were on the way to Europe.

But this was in 1908 — many years after the search was started.

Col. York took time away from his mourning to bring word to Leroy Dick that he and friends in Independence had raised a thousand dollars to post as reward money for information leading to the arrest of his brother's killers.

Reporters began arriving on the scene. Newspaper reporters from Kansas City, St. Louis, and Chicago were sent to cover the crime. Harper's Weekly, in New York, was represented by correspondents, photographers, and illustrators.

This was the same Harper's Weekly that carried weekly advertisements in the Thayer Headlight.

Harper's Weekly (Splendidly Illustrated)

Harper's Bazaar — a supplement to the Weekly — which carries full-sized patterns.

Harper's Magazine — with stories of travels all over the world.

The splendid illustrations were largely drawings made from photographs. Copies of those made at the murder scene were preserved in almost every collection pertaining to the Benders.

The Governor of Kansas, Thomas A. Osborn, issued a proclamation on May 17, 1873. He offered a reward of $2,000, $500 each, for the apprehension and delivery of John Bender, Mrs. Bender, John Bender, Jr., and Kate Bender.

Leroy Dick began receiving requests for information about the unidentified man. He would be called upon to exhume the body three times for possible identification.

The first request was from a woman in Canada whose missing husband had light hair and freckles. The shattered face and head kept identification from being made. Later a lady from England, who was sure she could identify her husband by a peculiarity about his teeth. The broken jaw and loosened teeth kept this from happening. The third disinterrment was for relatives of the missing Joe Sowers. These New Yorkers thought to make identification from the gold in the teeth, but once again, identification failed.

In the neighborhood and surrounding area, every conversation began and ended with the Benders.

People were called upon to tell their stories over and over again to reporters, fiction writers, and sensation seekers.

By June 25, the editor of the Thayer <u>Headlight</u> related in local news:

"...The whole of the house, excepting the heavy framing timbers on the Bender farm, and even the few trees, have been carried away by the relic hunters. The murderers themselves are probably in the middle of China by this time, and never will be heard from."

In the August 9 issue, the editor would report:

"...We visited the Bender scene and talked with Rudolph Brockman. He insists...no bodies, ...no arrests...The graves still remained unfilled."

In 1939, sixty-six years after the tragedy, Tom Collins, assistant to the publisher of the Kansas City <u>Journal</u>, came to Cherryvale to speak at the Community Picnic. In his column "This One's on Me," he prefaces his remarks by saying he had spent six months in the vicinity 20 years earlier compiling material for a 60,000 word story on the Benders for <u>The Journal</u>. He claimed that his employer took the completed story to New York and tentatively sold it to a syndicate for use as a serial feature. His boss, however, lost the story before completing the sale.

This was Collins' column, from the editorial page of the Kansas City <u>Journal</u>:

"There need never be any lack of conversational material in Cherryvale, Kas. I recently attended their annual soldiers' reunion and picnic and I found out a magic word still works.

"Just mention the name 'Bender' in or near Cherryvale and you've got conversation on your hands in quantities that you'll have trouble in stopping.

"As you probably know, the Benders, four of them, father, mother, daughter Kate and son John, ran a murder farm near Cherryvale in the early 1870's and made that Kansas town famous throughout the country and Europe.

"At least 11 persons, one of them a child, stopped at the hotel and store on the Parsons road, seven miles northeast of Cherryvale, and didn't return.

"The Benders slew their guests and robbed them and buried the corpses in the rear of the store, in an old apple orchard.

"The truth about the Benders was discovered after the disappearance of Dr. William York of Independence who was on his way to visit his brother, Col. A.M. York of Fort Scott.

"Twenty years ago I went to Cherryvale to talk with the five remaining men who were part of the posse that pursued the four fleeting Benders and write a complete story of that famous family and their crimes.

"The trouble was that each of the five eye-witnesses to the pursuit of the Benders told a different story.

"One fellow assured me that they got away. Another was equally positive that they all were hanged near the banks of a river. Both said they should know — they were there.

"The end of the Bender family was cloaked in mystery and it still is. All of those persons who lived in and near Cherryvale when the Benders operated there now are dead.

"But the argument still goes on. Approach any group in the fine park in that town and say, 'Bender' and you've got things started.

"The Santa Fe railroad ran special trains to Cherryvale so the morbidly curious could see the graves of the Bender victims.

"I saw a picture of one of the excursion specials once and people were clinging to the tops of the coaches which were packed to the windows.

"A Kansas City sheriff caught a Bender suspect, who turned out not to be the right man, and exhibited him at the old Gillis Theater at 25 cents a look.

"When they loaded the suspect on a train at the union depot to take to Cherryvale to be identified, people chinned themselves on the outside to peek in the windows at the supposed Bender.

"He retaliated and preserved his privacy by spitting tobacco juice in their eyes as they chinned on a level with the window.

"After nearly two-thirds of a century, I report that the Benders are not dead, in memory at least. They're still a live conversational topic in Cherryvale."

While the people of the immediate vicinity were coping with the notoriety thrust upon them, search for the killers was forging ahead.

Many unauthorized searches were held, with lynching fever afflicting every party. A band of Gypsies were accosted, stripped, their belongings ransacked for evidence. A Negro colony, squatters on the Territory line south of Coffeyville, was located. The "Bender detectives" rifled the tents, and upon finding some pieces of jewelry, started cuffing the woman and hooting at the feet of the men. Only intervention by some passing white men prevented bloodshed.

All that summer of 1873, self-appointed detectives held search parties over the area.

Col. York had seen the Benders only once, when

he talked to them about his brother's disappearance. He knew he would be unable to make positive identification, so begged Leroy Dick to give his assistance.

Leroy promised to do everything possible to be of help.

Peckham, Snoddy, and Beers agreed to use the reward money for their personal expenses, and set out on the trail.

When they made contact with the station manager at Humbolt, they learned that young John and Kate had switched trains there and gone south on the MKT. The old couple had continued on to Lawrence, where they bought tickets for St. Louis.

One could imagine the quarrelsome parting, as the spoils were divided. Some estimates at the time put the possible "take" as high as $50,000, which in those days was a considerable fortune.

At the St. Louis station a baggage agent remembered the doghide trunk and the white bundle. A drayman happened to be standing nearby, and commented that he had hauled that couple to an address in St. Louis. The odd trunk stayed in his mind, and also the difficulty he experienced finding where the old Dutchman wanted to go.

The detectives immediately went to the address given by the drayman. They discovered this to be the home of old John's sister.

She told the men that her brother and wife had, indeed, been at her home. She hadn't seen her brother for 20 years. He hadn't talked much in the week that he stayed at her home. She went out shopping one day and returned to find that they had left, without a word.

The men visited all the railroad stations and

checked out the river docks for any clues. They had reached another dead end, and were ready to concede defeat.

With the return to Kansas, they started checking all southeast Kansas railway lines. On the Frisco line they found a baggage master who remembered checking that particular trunk through to Vinita, Oklahoma.

They boarded the first train for Vinita.

Chapter 7

•◄◄◉►►•

As the detectives were en route to Vinita, Leroy Dick was handed a startling clue. Albert H. Owen, a boarding house proprietor near Denison, Texas, came to Parsons with a remarkable story. Milt Reynolds in Parsons brought Owen out to Leroy's place in his carriage.

The story Owen told sent all three men racing back to Parsons to wire the latest development to Peckham, Snoddy, and Beers in Vinita.

Owen told his listeners that a big railroad gang was doing grading near his boarding house, and many of the men were lodging with him. A wiry young German got a job and pitched a tent nearby. He was living there with his wife — and an old couple came to see them.

The young man told Owen that they were leaving — to locate with his folks in Texas. Owen responded that there was a lot of good cattle range farther down.

The young German indicated that his folks wanted to go farther west — to a colony they had heard of near the border.

Owen knew the young fellow was talking about an outlaw colony down there. He warned the young man that it was a dangerous place — full of desperate criminals hiding from the law.

The man's parents wanted to settle close by the colony and raise vegetables and have dairy products to sell to the outlaws.

Owen warned him again that it was a cutthroat group. He told of an incident when he had been a deputy sheriff and had gone after a killer there. He and his chief had felt lucky to get away with their lives.

The problem was, he explained, that the border line between Texas and New Mexico was uncertain. Only a rough survey had been made. Lawmen in each state were waiting for the other to clean out the den.

Owen told another incident, reinforcing the dangers of getting near the outlaws.

None of the warnings seemed to affect the young section hand. Before noon the following morning he and his folks left, in the boy's wagon, which he had ready for the purpose.

Leroy wired Peckham and Beers at Vinita, and learned that Marshal Snoddy had returned to his duties in Ft. Scott. The other two arranged to meet Owen at Denison and get a description of John's team and wagon.

A return wire from Peckham and Beers told Leroy that the two had bought some ponies and a camping outfit, and had located the Benders' trail.

The trail led the two men about two hundred miles west of Denison. Then the ranches became thousands of acres in size, habitations were widely scattered and isolated, and trails angled off in many directions. The searchers lost all track of the Benders, and resorted to traveling southwest.

They picked up the trail of the Benders at a ranch house and trailed them to El Paso. There they hired a Mexican guide and crossed the border into Mexico. The trail ended. They re-crossed the Red River and started back north.

North of El Paso, they stopped at another ranch house and once again picked up the trail. A cowhand remembered the four German speaking travelers. He had guided them to a spot where they could find their way to the outlaw colony.

The cowhand added more information about the colony. The criminals lived there, in a timbered area, in tents and huts and dug-outs. He said the two searchers' lives would be over if they tried to go in after the killers.

Peckham and Beers gave up the chase. They sold their ponies in a railroad town, and returned by rail to Kansas.

Leroy Dick and Col. York were keenly disappointed. They felt strongly that the Texas Rangers should wipe out the criminals' den. Leroy sent a wire to Austin with the request. His answer from there was that Ft. Sill would be the proper place to contact.

Inquiry at Ft. Sill produced the same results. There was no knowledge of the extent of the colony, no funds available for a survey of state boundaries.

This seemed the end of the chase. Life would go back to normal, and the Benders would never be heard of again.

Of course there would be no return to normal. Sensation seekers continued to come to view the murder plot. Letters arrived from relatives in the

East, trying to get information about their loved ones.

Some of the families whose names had been linked with the Benders sold their claims and moved away.

Rudolph Brockman must have married in a year or two after Kate's disappearance. He and his first wife produced four children before the wife's death in 1881 — and Kate disappeared only eight years before that. Rudolph didn't pine for Kate very long.

While the active searches had ceased, and the principals in the drama were trying to get on with their lives, fate was at work in the lives of the criminals.

Unknown to the Big Hill characters in the story, the four murderers were again parting ways. The old couple tired of life with the outlaws, and decided to go back to Michigan. The young couple was not ready to go, and Kate and John demanded their split of the money. A fight broke out between the two men, and the women were hard put to break it up.

The old couple left, with Pa still in possession of the loot.

That night he and Ma camped in the mountains near Denver. He left Ma building a fire while he went to town for provisions. Ma finally caught on that he wasn't coming back.

Being deserted was no problem for Ma. When she learned that old man Bender had bought a ticket on the Union Railroad for points East, she put up such a pitiful story that the citizens of the town raised money to pay her way back to Michigan. Not so hard to imagine, when you consider that she charmed twelve men into marriage in her life of crime.

She had several children living in Michigan. She visited them — and kept her guard up for word about old John — and the money.

Meanwhile — back in the outlaw colony, Kate wanted to go home to Michigan. Young John refused. A young painter drifted into the colony — stayed a while — and disappeared. In a few days Kate, too, disappeared.

When next we hear of Kate, she and the painter had wandered to McPherson, Kansas.

In McPherson, Kate and the painter were frightfully poor. Kate would borrow her neighbor's washing machine to do her laundry. On one of her borrowing sessions she was in a bad humor and complained to the neighbor, Mrs. McCann, that the damned ol' woman Bender had brought her to that point. At Mrs. McCann's gasp, she answered recklessly that the old woman was her mother. When Mrs. McCann got interested, she refused to say any more.

In the ensuing conversation, Mrs. McCann told the particulars of the orphanage, and Kate showed a wary interest.

Some time later Kate became ill with a fever. The painter had deserted her, and Mrs. McCann took on the job as volunteer nurse.

While Kate was in delirium, she told her nurse over and over again that she knew things about her — that she could tell who she was.

When Kate was on trial, a few years later, her lawyer would tell how Mrs. McCann had planted all of these ideas in Kate's mind, through use of a magnet, which "magnetized" her, and put Kate in McCann's absolute control.

Kate recovered, and was anxious about what she had revealed. Mrs. McCann evaded by saying that she had called the Benders "wonderfully smart people."

When Kate had recovered her strength, she told Mrs. McCann a story about her identity. In Kate's story, the woman's parents lived in Windsor, Canada. A woman and her 16 year old daughter came to nurse McCann's mother through her confinement. When the daughter fell in love with the young father-to-be and he refused to reciprocate, the 16-year-old took a knife, went to the cellar, and lured the young man down to his death. The young mother died in a few days — supposedly of childbirth.

In the story, the nurse took the baby (Mrs. McCann) and her daughter and moved to Kentucky until the affair had blown over. They then took the baby to the orphanage in Iowa and left her there.

Mrs. McCann begged Kate to tell the names of the nurse and of her parents, but Kate claimed to have forgotten completely. In several days Kate packed her belongings and vowed her intention of going to Michigan to get her share of the money.

With Kate's departure, Frances McCann became so distraught that she was a woman obsessed. All her life she had yearned to know about her parents. Now she felt she must go to Michigan and search out the truth. She told her husband that they must be made to pay for the murders of her parents.

Her husband asked who <u>they</u> were.

Frances told him that she was convinced Ma Bender was the murderess. She could not rest until she had exhausted every lead.

Mr. McCann was also an orphan, and he gave his wife his blessing, and helped her make her journeys.

Frances McCann traveled to Michigan and had no difficulty finding stories of a lewd character named Mrs. Almira Griffith, who, with her daughter, Mary, had been run out of several logging camps. Frances was convinced that this was the same person as old Mrs. Bender.

Mrs. McCann came home and started a series of letter writing, to get information. No length of time is given for the collection of evidence that was being made.

Frances went back to Michigan a second time. She learned that Mrs. Griffith had been born Almira Meik in the Adirondacks. She had grown into a large, healthy woman with a mean disposition and a violent temper. Married to a small, weakly man, she had borne twelve sons and daughters.

Frances McCann learned that her own mother had been Almira Griffith's oldest child. Second was the daughter, Mary, who had inherited her mother's ungodly temperament. Then came Flora, a son, William, Eliza, whose name would be known as Kate, a boy and girl who died in infancy, a boy afflicted with "fits", Clara, Myra, Ella, and another who died young. At the time of the murder of Mrs. McCann's parents, the family was living in Windsor, Canada, just across the river from Detroit.

Kate had been telling the truth when she told the story of the flight to Kentucky, and the subsequent placing of the baby in the orphanage in Iowa.

When Almira later testified in the case she brought against her daughter, Kate, she told the court a tender story. She had married George Griffith when she was only fourteen or fifteen. He was a small, fragile man, afflicted with bouts of quinsy. An ax handle maker by trade. When her youngest child was just a baby, Mr. Griffith was rocking the cradle and Almira asked him to get some wood. He got up and fell and hit his head on the cradle, and died right there.

Almira should have put credence in the immortal

lines, "The mills of the gods grind slow, but they grind exceeding fine..." Who could imagine that, a few years after that testimony, Leroy Dick would meet, in Parsons, Jim Mapes, who had been a neighbor of the Griffiths in Ionia. Mapes helped dress Griffith's body for burial. He and the other men found a bad place on Griffith's head, it looked like the dent of an ax handle. The men decided the wife had flown into a rage and struck him a fatal blow. They made no accusations.

This revelation was one of the long progressions of incidents that fit together in an uncanny pattern — almost as if an unseen finger were pointing the way.

Frances McCann returned to Kansas with the certainty that the unholy Almira Griffith — old Mrs. John Bender — was her very own grandmother.

Chapter 8

•◄◄●►►•

A t the time Frances McCann was relentlessly
following every lead, Leroy Dick had moved
his family to Parsons. He found work there
helping to put a stone floor in the stockyards. He was
convinced that the Benders were still quartered in the
outlaw colony of Texas.

Mrs. McCann had not lessened her quest for
vengeance. If the old woman did, indeed, prove to be
Frances' own grandmother, all the more reason she
should be brought to justice.

Frances McCann made her third trip to Michigan.
Authorities there were as eager to put Almira and her
daughter, Kate, behind bars as was Mrs. McCann.
They offered her assistance whenever she asked.

On the third trip Mrs. McCann learned that old
John Bender had been confined in a Presbyterian
hospital with a serious illness. Mrs. Bender had
traced him there and begged to be allowed to visit
him. As she sat waiting in the visitor's lounge, old
John approached from the rear, caught sight of his
unexpected visitor, and fell in a dead faint. Mrs.

Bender made a hurried departure, rather than to risk questioning. A while later the old man disappeared from the hospital.

Mrs. McCann discovered other valuable information for Labette County authorities on this third trip in 1888. She came back to Parsons and tried to get officials to go to Michigan and gather information to prosecute the two women.

The county attorney sent Mrs. McCann to see Leroy Dick. He found her story fantastic, and totally unbelievable. He assured Frances McCann that it was a case of mistaken identity — that he was convinced the Benders had never left the Texas colony.

Mrs. McCann would not concede defeat. She stood firm in her convictions. In 1889 she made a fourth trip to Michigan, and this time brought home what she felt was incontestable evidence. She took this to Bill Porter, the county treasurer, who was impressed in spite of himself.

Again Frances McCann would be sent to talk to Leroy Dick. He remained unconvinced — sure that the Benders would not risk leaving the outlaw colony.

Mrs. McCann told Leroy that the two women were in jail in Berrien Springs, Michigan, awaiting trial. She knew them to be the Benders, and pleaded with Leroy to go up and make positive identification. Leroy stood just as firm, and protested that he could not leave his job.

Sheriff Wilson became persuaded of Mrs. McCann's story. He felt too old to make the trip, but his son, Bud, was eager to go. Bud took the photograph of the old woman, given to him by Mrs. McCann, to several old neighbors in the mound district. When they identified it as Mrs. Bender, Sheriff Wilson appointed Bud to bring the Benders to justice, and made out the papers in his name.

Mrs. McCann objected. She knew that Bud was not acquainted with the women and could not make identification. She took her case to the county attorney, who called Leroy to his office.

Leroy went — in a furious mood. He straightened the attorney out on the reasons why he had no intention of going. The attorney changed the subject and told Leroy his wife had a lot of pictures of nice old ladies, and he would like to see if Leroy knew any of them.

When the pictures were spread out, Leroy picked up one in surprise, and said it was old Mrs. Bender.

The county attorney told him it was a photograph of Almira Griffith. He insisted that Dick must go to Michigan and investigate. He asked how much money Leroy would need.

It was arranged for Leroy to travel under the name of Bud Wilson, using the papers already made out. This was done to keep from alerting the women and prosecutors that someone from Kansas was investigating.

A telegraph was sent to the Berrien county officers, and Leroy traveled to Niles, a small logging community where he talked with the county attorney. With full cooperation assured, he went on to Berrien and met with Sheriff Wrenn.

The sheriff told Leroy that the old woman and her daughters were a bad lot. They had been kicked out of many logging communities — but never had been convicted of any crimes, because of lack of evidence. He said that the law officers thought they had something to pin on Flora, the third daughter. She was thought to be the weakling, who might be persuaded to talk. Flora disappeared, and the officers were sure that the old lady had killer her, but nothing could be proved. In light of the later discoveries about murders committed by the old woman, disposal of another daughter would not be a concern.

The sheriff confirmed that Bender was only an assumed name for the criminals, than none of them had the actual name of Bender, and that the only family relationship was between Ma and Kate.

Leroy asked what charges the officers were able to use to bring the women to trial.

It seems that Ma got wind of Frances McCann's fourth visit, and how close her investigation was coming to the real truth. Ma was living, at that time, in a little shack close to Niles. Kate had just married her seventh husband, taken her children, and moved out. Thinking to throw Kate to the law as the actual Kate Bender and escape consequences herself, Ma came to the officers and asked to have Kate arrested for stealing.

"What did she steal from you?"

"A frying pan — some pewter plates — some baby stockings."

Kate (Eliza) was arrested, brought to trial, and swore her mother gave her the objects. The sheriff said the trial was a mere sham, and they had to release the women.

When word came to the sheriff that Mrs. McCann had instituted charges, the sheriff trailed them up on the St. Joe River and brought them back to jail. Kate (Eliza) swore her mother tried to kill her several times on the river trip.

The sheriff was going to make his nightly rounds of the jail, and asked Leroy to go along to see if he recognized the women.

When Leroy hesitated about a confrontation before he was ready, the sheriff explained a plan for concealment.

As Leroy watched, hidden on the stairway, the old woman turned in his direction, and identification was certain, complete to clumsy, rolling motion, and peculiar squint.

The following day Sheriff Wrenn took Leroy to Buchanan, White Pigeon, and Three Rivers on an unsuccessful search for evidence.

That evening he introduced Leroy to the women as Mr. Wilson, a county commissioner from St. Joseph. The old woman asked for a private talk with Leroy.

She explained to him that she wanted a private cell — she was afraid of her daughter. She was a bad girl — would lie, steal — might even try to poison her. She confided that Eliza was actually the famous Kate Bender — then pulled a clipping about the murders out of her stocking.

Leroy promised to use his influence.

When they returned to the others, Eliza asked for her turn in private.

She picked up her little girl and went into the storeroom. Leroy must help her get a private cell. Her mother was trying to kill her — and her child. Had already tried to poison her once. The reason? Her mother was actually Kate Bender — had a part in those Bender murders in Kansas.

Leroy promised to use his influence.

When they had joined the others, Leroy threw his punch line — that he remembered Kate from his singing school back in Harmony Grove.

Each of the women protested vigorously that all she knew of the murders was the other telling her about them.

Sheriff Wrenn and Leroy took Kate, her mother and the baby from the jail in Berrien Springs to the courthouse in Niles for Kate's trial for theft.

The district attorney put Ma on the stand first. He asked how much value she placed on the stolen items. When she answered fifty cents would cover it, a laugh went around the room.

Kate, called to the stand, answered that the charge was a lie — that her mother simply wanted to get her mixed up in the Bender scrape.

Almira broke in with the accusation that Kate was that person, and the two shouted at one another.

The lawyer brought Almira back to the stand, and unfolded an incredible history about her. Almira apparently enjoyed every moment of her performance. The spectators, too, seemed to feel this crude old woman as a comic figure. Mrs. McCann, listening unobtrusively from the back, found no humor in the tale.

The lawyer elicited the information that Almira had married George Griffith and bore him twelve children. He dropped dead when her youngest child was a baby. She had married a logger near Grass Lake. They drifted apart. Then she married a logger at Jackson and someone else at Dowagiac. She married two different men at St. Joseph, another at Flint, another at Saginaw, another at Muskegon. Twelve in all. When the judge remarked that she had been muchly married, she told him with a smirk, that she was still in the market.

This brought a big laugh from the crowd. What a funny old woman.

When the lawyer tried to connect her with a German, she stoutly denied it, and stuck to her story.

Leroy went to a couple of logging camps mentioned by Almira. He found no evidence of any marriage, but did add to her background. He learned that the oldest boy, William, had brought his pregnant wife to the family home in Ionia. One morning when the boy had gone to work, Almira flew into a rage, struck the young wife a blow that killed her and the unborn child. She was convicted of murder and sentenced to 19 years in the penitentiary. She served 17 months, and was freed through the efforts of an unscrupulous lawyer.

When the trial resumed, the same territory was covered, with the two women constantly shouting out against one another.

Kate (Eliza) being recalled to the stand, claimed her mother had been trying to take her life since she was a kid. When asked why, Kate's story was that a little colored girl had come to play with her younger sisters when the family moved to Ionia. One day Almira had flown into a murderous rage and killed the little girl. She concealed the body until night, put the body in a horse-drawn cart, made Kate go with her, and drove out to a deep hole in a swamp or slough, and dumped the kid in. She threatened that if Kate ever told about it, she would kill her, too.

The Mr. Mapes in Parsons, who had lived in Ionia, remembered the swamp and that there was a deep hole there that never went dry.

On the next evening's search for evidence, Leroy and the sheriff turned up more background on this murderous old woman.

Near Dowagiac they found that Almira and her oldest daughters had been run out of the logging camp for baby farming and other revolting practices. Almira had moved in with a farmer, taking only her boy who had "fits." The farmer disappeared a little later. Almira mourned for him loudly and publicly, then advertised a sale of his farm, stock, and personal property. With a tidy sum from this sale, she prepared to move to Niles.

A couple of hunters stopped at the farm for a drink from the well. They spotted a coat floating on the surface. When the body was pulled out, it was the missing farmer.

At Almira's arrest, her boy, epileptic, was confined in the same cell with her. She protested, saying he couldn't stand confinement, and had to have a doctor quickly.

The doctor came quickly, that night, to the cell, and was helpless, as the boy died in terrible agony. With the only witness gone, Almira was again freed. The body count was growing.

The following day in court, when the lawyer threw this new accusation at her, Almira was saddened by the thought. It was mean of people to say that about her. The farmer husband, had been a good old man.

"I wouldn't a-harmed a hair on his head."

Kate disagreed. She said that her mother poisoned her own son, in jail, for fear that he would break down under cross-examination.

Now it was time to question Kate's sister, Clara. Leroy traced her to a little town across an inlet. He kept his assumed identity of County Commissioner Wilson. Clara said she would not lie about her mother's whereabouts in '70 and '71 — had no idea where she was living then.

Did she remember her mother ever marrying a German?

Oh, sure, she remembered him. The reason she remembered was because she, Clara, had brought herself home a pretty little fella, and her ma had taken him by the neck and throwed him out in the street. The German was there that day.

Could she describe him?

Looked mean and gruff — like he wanted to kill somebody. Rough old cheek bones — shaggy hair. Dark brown hair. His eyebrows were so bushy she couldn't tell the color of his eyes.

Like all the descriptions ever given of old John Bender.

After suffering through several dirty yarns, and bringing Clara back again and again to the subject, Leroy finally prodded her memory enough to produce a name — John Flickinger.

Leroy caught a train to St. Joseph, a town mentioned frequently in the trial.

Again there were no licensed records. The authorities confirmed that they were ready to prosecute Flora, Kate, and Clara for baby farming. Then Flora disappeared.

Leroy went across the river to Benton Harbor. Here was the sanitorium where Mrs. Bender had traced her sick husband.

The authorities there knew nothing about the man, but Leroy struck up a conversation with a man in the hotel lobby, asked if he had ever heard of John Flickinger, and, once more had a missing piece of the puzzle.

The man described old John Bender right down to the crooked little finger on his hand. John Bender (Flickinger) had been in the sanitorium there.

The speaker said that earlier in the same year of the conversation ('89) he had roomed at the boarding house where Flickinger stayed. One morning Flickinger didn't come down to breakfast. The story teller went on to work at his job turning over logs in a mill pond. About noon he turned over a log and a man's body bobbed up. It was Flickinger, and the verdict was suicide.

Leroy took his latest finding back to the sheriff and district attorney. They were sure they now had a convincing case. They promised to send the women to Kansas without requisition, to save expenses on all sides.

The courtroom on that day was packed with spectators. Kate and her ma had to be called to order time and again in order to complete the cross-examination.

At last the attorney sprang his newest surprise. He threw at Almira the name of her German husband — John Flickinger.

Almira, for once, was dumbfounded. She gasped and stared, and then recovered her insolence. Yes, she guessed she did have Flickinger. Why did she forget? Oh, because she had so many. But that did not say she wasn't still in the market.

This time the laughter had worn thin.

The trial was over — and the women were set free.

The sheriff said later that the whole trial was a farce, and a waste of the taxpayers' money.

Chapter 9

◄━◄━●━►━►

Leroy had been furiously making plans to take the women back to Kansas. He kept his identity secret, because there had been talk by the mayor and others that if anyone from Kansas came up, he would be detained, and the trial would be conducted there in Niles, which would bring many people to town, and put them on the map. Leroy knew the trial must be held in Kansas.

A deputy had been appointed to keep track of the two women overnight. There was no train out until the next morning. Leroy gave himself the barest margin to get the women aboard, because he knew if the mayor learned of the departure, he would serve a subpoena, and Leroy Dick would be detained in Niles.

The next morning the deputy brought Kate and her baby to Berrien Springs, and the men went after Ma, who had spent the night at the home of her daughter, Myra. Myra was living with an Italian.

They found Almira still in bed. She was told to get her clothes on and come with the men. She burst into profanity and screamed that she would not go. She appealed to the Italian, who told her he could do nothing. She and the Italian cursed at each other.

Leroy told her if she didn't get some clothes on, he would take her in her old wrapper, and take her back to Kansas in chains.

When they arrived at the station, where the crowd had gathered, the old woman thought of a new tactic. She pulled the hat from her head, threw it under the train, and refused to go a damned step back to Kansas without a new bonnet. A woman in the crowd took $6.00 from Leroy, hurried to town, and came back with a new bonnet before the train pulled out.

The news about the arrest had traveled far and fast. At all major stops Leroy was besieged by reporters — from New York, Philadelphia, Cincinnati, Richmond. At Indianapolis his brother Temple and his wife caught sight of the women as the train pulled in, and cried, "There's Kate Bender!" and, "Yes, the old woman, too."

This was before Leroy had even appeared. Going on to St. Louis, other reporters kept popping up from Chicago and other midland towns.

Leroy was surrounded by reporters at St. Louis, Sedalia, and Ft. Scott. As they rolled along out of Nevada, Missouri, Kate came up to Leroy and told him he shouldn't think she was without friends. She wouldn't be in Kansas two hours before there would be a good lawyer to defend her.

A reporter sitting close by remarked, after she had gone, that she had a pretty little baby, and wasn't that surprising.

Leroy had mentioned the same thing to Kate's sister, Clara, back in Michigan. Clara had laughed and told him Eliza did have a child, but didn't like it, so got rid of it, and when the cops got wise, hunted up another kid to hush up the investigation. Clara had no idea where Eliza found the child.

Morrison and Sheriff Wilson had been notified of the arrival, so they would be prepared for the preliminary hearing. Leroy had also been in touch with his father so that the neighbors still living in the Big Hill area could be summoned as witnesses.

While arrangements were being made for the testimony, a well dressed young man appeared, spoke with the women as one who was acquainted with them, and leaned over the baby to talk to Kate.

This man would prove to be the lawyer for the defense — with a marked resemblance to Kate's baby.

In the book written by this young lawyer some twenty years later, about the trial, he would introduce himself as John T. James, lately of Minneapolis, Minnesota.

Leroy listed the names of those summoned as witnesses: Father Dienst, Maurice Sparks, Rudolph Brockman, Ben Ferguson, his brother Temple, his sister, Mrs. Delilah Keck, Jim McMain, Bob Campbell, Bob's brother-in-law, Tom Finley, Henry McKean, William McCramb, and himself.

Of those questioned about recognition of the two women, seven answered, "Yes," six answered that they looked the same, but the witnesses could not swear to the fact. Rudolph Brockman said that he didn't know. When asked to swear that they were not, he burst out, "No, by golly. I don't swear they ain't."

This was in November, 1889, and the women were bound over to the district courts for trial in May of the following year.

A warrant for their arrest was issued by the state of Kansas, to the Sheriff, or any Constable of Labette County. The warrant had been issued on August 12, 1889 — apparently in the event that Mrs. McCann's investigation should bear fruit. The warrant was for the arrest of John Bender, senior, Kate Bender, senior, Kate Bender, junior, and John Bender, Jr. It was filed to direct the sheriff or constable to arrest these parties and bring them before the law.

This warrant was filed on January 9, 1890. The warrant is on file at the court house in Oswego, Kansas.

It contains such gross inaccuracies as a description of Wm. York's murder taking place on June 15, 1872, and his languishing overnight, until he died on June 16, 1872. The heavy iron hammer was stated to be held by John Bender, Sr. This is the only charge of murder brought against the four.

Why this document would so falsify the date of York's murder is incomprehensible, since the time of the doctor's disappearance, in March of 1873, was well established in countless records of the time.

The women were no sooner bound over than they began again their bickering, fighting, and complaints against each other. As always, they were convincing, and quarters were found for them away from the jail — in a private home.

How did they deceive so many people? Even with conclusive evidence against them for numerous vile acts, people of Oswego felt concerned — to the extent of purchasing a maternity outfit for Kate when she put out a false story of pregnancy.

A precipe for subpoena was filed on January 30, 1890, against Almira Griffith, alias Kate Bender, Sr.

and Sarah E. Davis alias Kate Bender, Jr. for the offense of murder in the first degree.

On the 5th day of February, 1890, subpoenas were issued to a number of witnesses to appear in court.

In lawyer John T. James' account of the trial proceedings, he spoke with compelling ardor about the pitiful case of his two clients being held, penniless, far from home and friends, with no way to prove their innocence.

The verdict was in doubt. The women continued to be held.

Leroy received a bit of shocking news. The Parsons chief of police told him both women had been set free. Leroy wouldn't believe it — told the chief he was crazy.

The policeman told him that he, the chief, had seen them that very morning on foot, pulling Kate's baby in an express wagon. He said, to make things worse, well-meaning people in Parsons had raised money to get them to Ft. Scott.

An incredulous Leroy Dick went to Judge Keesy for confirmation. He demanded to know what right anyone had to set the wholesale murderers free.

The judge said the expenses of the indictment had cost the county so much, and the conviction would cost so much more, that taxes would be boosted way up.

Leroy protested that this was insufficient reason to free the two. The judge told him then about a marriage certificate that had been received. The good-looking young lawyer for the defense had turned up in Oswego with a certificate of marriage of Almira Griffith to a Mr. James at Jackson, Michigan, in 1872.

Leroy cried out in protest. He told the judge that

he had examined all of the records in Jackson and there wasn't a scratch about her marrying anyone. The certificate had to be a fake.

The judge shrugged, and said the lawyer maintained it was authentic. There was nothing to do but dismiss the women.

About a month after they had been freed, Leroy read in the Parsons Sun that Labette County and Leroy Dick were being sued for the sum of $10,000.

Leroy sped to Oswego and consulted Dick Mason. He learned that Kate and the old woman had come down from Ft. Scott and filed suit, for damages to the peace and reputation of Almira Griffith.

Leroy was full of indignation. As he rushed out of the office, he ran headlong into the two women, pulling the baby in the express wagon.

He stormed and raved at the two. Kate told him he had caused them a lot of trouble. Now it was his turn. They had to do something — they were destitute.

The old woman said piously that she had warned Kate not to try to injure the reputation of a nice, respectable family man.

Kate screamed back at her, and Leroy walked away in disgust. His last view of them was as they straggled down the sidewalk, fighting with one another.

The suit against Leroy Dick was dropped when the young lawyer appeared and told Kate to get out of town, or she would land in the pen. He said he had gotten her out of one mess, but had gone his limit.

Why did the countless tales of the Benders leave their ending in mystery? Why did the authors choose one of the many confessions telling of vigilante justice polishing off the murderers?

Leroy Dick and Frances McCann did not complete their investigation until 16 years after the discovery of the bodies in the orchard.

Except for sporadic tales spun by the "penny dreadfuls," reporters had given up on the story. That many years, with no arrests, and no payment of rewards, had led most people to the conclusion that at least one of the deathbed accounts of the Benders' execution by a posse must be true.

Even a news item telling about Col. York visiting the area from his home in Denver, many years later, changed the minds of very few. The newspaper account quoted Col. York as maintaining his strong conviction that no one put and end to the Benders.

All of the principal characters in the tragedy are gone now. The evidence remaining is found in the court records at Oswego, the murder hammers behind glass in the Cherryvale Museum, the hundreds of thousands of words in print, and the memories of the area residents who heard the stories first-hand from their relatives.

A Kansas Historical marker tells the story to travelers along highway 160, between Parsons and Cherryvale. Nothing of any kind remains to show the spot on the prairie where the Bender Inn once stood, and where the orchard yielded its grisly secret.

Somewhere, in the descendants of those people living nearby when the tragedy unfolded, are other bits and pieces of this section of history — the silenced eight-day clock, the canes made from the walnut table, pieces of wood torn from the house, pages of Kate's journal left strewn about, the abandoned wagon, and the shotgun, pieces of jewelry taken from the victims.

And somewhere, too, must be the recording of the

death and burial of one Almira Griffith, and one Sara Eliza Davis. Did Baby Girl James of the flaxen hair and the laughing eyes survive — to make her escape from the little express wagon? Yet today, it is possible to walk down the street and brush unwittingly against a descendant of those two long ago murderers.

Dullix, ix, ux...

LABETTE COUNTY DISTRICT COURT

No. 925   Page 362

State of Kansas

Against

John Bender, Sen.
Kate Bender, Sen.
Kate Bender, Jr.
and John Bender, Jr.
            Defendants

Filed January 9, 1890
Colin Hodge, Clerk
J.H. Morrison
        Atty for Plaintiff

The state of Kansas, to the Sheriff or any Constable of Labette County
Whereas, complaint in writing under oath, has been made to me, and it appearing that there are reasonable grounds for believing that on the 15th day of June, 1872, in Labette County and state of Kansas, John Bender, Sr., Kate Bender, Sr., wife of the said John Bender, Sr., Kate Bender, Jr. and John Bender, Jr. did then and unlawfully, feloniously, with force and arms in and upon one Wm. York, wilfully, deliberately, premeditatedly, and with malice aforethought, did make an assault and said John

Bender, Sr., Kate Bender, Sr., wife of said John Bender, Sr., Kate Bender, Jr., and John Bender, Jr., did then and there with a certain heavy iron hammer, a deadly weapon, held in the hands of the said John Bender, Sr., aided, abetted, and assisted by the said Kate Bender, Sr., Kate Bender, Jr., and John Bender, Jr., purposely, wilfully, and deliberately, premeditatedly, unlawfully, and feloniously strike the said Wm. York, then and there with the iron hammer aforesaid, one mortal wound, of which said mortal wound the said Wm. York from the 15th day of June, AD 1872, until the 16th day of June, AD 1872, did suffer and languish, and languishing did live; on which said 16th day of June, AD 1872, in the county aforesaid, the said Wm. York of the said mortal would did die, and so the said John Bender, Sr., Kate Bender, Sr., wife of said John Bender, Sr., Kate Bender, Jr., and John Bender, Jr., in manner and form aforesaid, did wilfully, deliberately, premeditatedly, unlawfully, and feloniously and of deliberate and premeditated malice aforethought kill and murder the said Wm. York, contrary to the statues in such case made and provided against the peace and dignity of the state of Kansas.

You are therefore commanded, forthwith, to arrest said John Bender, Sr., Kate Bender, Sr., wife of said John Bender, Sr., Kate Bender, Jr., and John Bender, Jr., and bring them before some magistrate of and within said County to be dealt with according to law. And then and there return this writ.

Witness my hand, at my office in the City of Oswego in said County, this 23rd day of August, 1889.

> E.D. Kinsey
> Justice of the Peace.

On back of the Warrant:

State of Kansas, County of Labette, S.S.

Rec'd this warrant on the 23rd of August, 1889, and executed the same Nov. 2nd, 1889 by arresting the within named Kate Bender, Sr. and Kate Bender, Jr. and bringing them before the within named Justice of the Peace Oswego to Niles 714 miles and returning 800 miles = 1514 miles at 10 cents

per mile =	$151.40
Making arrests	1.00
1,000 miles extra travel in securing proof	100.00
800 miles on Kate Bender, Sr. at 5 cents per mile	40.00
800 miles on Kate Bender, Jr. at 5 cents per mile	40.00
Total	322.40
W.P. Wilson, Sheriff attendance	1.00

By D.H. Wilson, Sheriff

ORDER OF DISAPPEARANCES OF VICTIMS

JOE SOWERS - (not proved to be a victim) 1869

MR. JONES - body discovered in Drum Creek in May, 1871

TWO UNKNOWN MEN FOUND ON PRAIRIE - after blizzard of Feb., 1872

HENRY McKENZIE - November 6th or 7th, 1872

BEN BROWN - late in 1872

W.F. McCROTTY - late in 1872

JOHN GREARY - ?

GEORGE LONCHER AND LITTLE GIRL - February or early March, 1873

DR. WILLIAM YORK March 9, 1873

MONEY TAKEN FROM VICTIMS

BOYLE $1,900
McCROTTY $2,600
BROWN $36 Finely matched team
McKENZIE $2,000 or 40 cents (depending on
    source used)
LONCHER $38
DR. YORK $10 red pacing mare, saddle (or $800 to
    $900, depending on source)
When JOHN GREARY was listed as a victim, he was
said to be carrying $2,000.

ORDER OF DISCOVERY OF GRAVES

1. DR. YORK   Tuesday
2. HENRY McKENZIE   Wednesday
3. W.F. McCROTTY   Wednesday
4. UNIDENTIFIED MAN   Wednesday
5. BEN BROWN   Wednesday
6. GEORGE LONCHER AND LITTLE
    GIRL   Wednesday
7. JOHNNY BOYLE (in well)   Wednesday

NOT VERIFIED:
    JOHN GREARY
    UNKNOWN FEMALE

MAJOR POINTS OF DISAGREEMENT

GEORGE LONCHER, LOOCHER, LORCHER, LOUNCHER, LONGCORS

AGE OF DAUGHTER:
18 months
3 years old
5 years old
child of 7 or 8
10 or 12 years

NUMBER OF BODIES
FOUND:
8 bodies
no doubt 11 were dug up in
    orchard
9 men, one woman, little girl,
plus dismembered parts of
several victims

BIBLIOGRAPHY

PUBLISHED SOURCES

A History of Montgomery County, Alderman, Robert H., The Bloody Benders, Stein and Day, New York, 1970

Case, Nelson, "History of Parsons", in History of Labette County, Kansas, Chicago Biographical Publishing Co., 1901

Graves, W.W., Life and Letters of Fathers of Osage Mission, 1916

Hardy, Allison, Kate Bender, The Kansas Murderess, Girard, Kansas, Haldeman-Julius Publication, 1944

Harper, Paul, Surely It Floweth With Milk and Honey, Independence Community College Press, 1988, pp. 25, 26, 91-98, 99-108

Isely, Bliss, and Richards, W.M., Four Centuries of Kansas. Wichita, Kansas, The McCormick Mathers Company, 1936

James, John T., The Benders in Kansas, Wichita, Kansas, Kan-Okla Publishing Company, 1913

Nixon, Ruth, History of Big Hill and Old Mount Zion, 1982

Socolofsky, Homer, and Self, Huber, Historical Atlas of Kansas, 2nd Edition, University of Oklahoma Press, 1972, 1988

Wellman, Manly Wade, <u>Candle of the Wicked</u>, G.P. Putnam's Sons, no date

Worley, J.D., <u>The Bender Family</u>, Cherryvale Republican Press, 1899

PERIODICALS

<u>Argosy</u>, February, 1967, "The Case of the Prairie Siren" Downing, Jim, "Bloody Benders", <u>Midweek</u>, feature magazine of the <u>Tulsa Tribune</u>, Sept. 14, 1977

Harris, John P., "Beautiful Katie", <u>Kansas Magazine</u>, 1936

Hynd, Alan, "Mistress of Murder", <u>True Police</u>, 1960

Montgomery, Wayne, "Self-Styled Devil's Disciple", <u>True Frontier</u>, June, 1972

Rozar, Lily B., "Bloody Benders of Kansas", <u>Pioneer West</u>, April, 1970

"The Benders", <u>Kansas Magazine</u>, September 1886, pp. 254-55

<u>The Little Balkans Review</u>, "The Benders Hills Mystery", Leroy Dick, as told to Jean McEwen, Little Balkans Press, Spring, 1983, Summer, 1983, Fall, 1983, Winter 1983-84, Spring 1984, Summer, 1984, Fall-Winter 1984-85, Winter 1988-89

FROM THE ARCHIVES OF THE KANSAS STATE HISTORICAL SOCIETY

Independence <u>Tribune</u>, microfilm, January, 1873, to April, 1873, copies missing from April to July, 1873

Ross, Edith Connelly, <u>The Bloody Benders</u>, Wichita, Kansas, KansasState Historical Society Collections, 1962-68, Vol. XVII, 15 pp.

Thayer <u>Headlight</u>, microfilm, years 1871 through 1873

NEWSPAPERS

Bohlander, Frank, "Trail Road Goes Unmarked", Independence <u>Reporter</u>, July 14, 1961

Brown, Connie, "Accounts Differ on Fate of Bender Family", Parsons <u>Sun</u>, October 18, 1989

Coffey, Ivy, "Death at Dinnertime", date between 1961 and 1967

Dick, Leroy F., as told to McEwen, Jean, "The Bender Hills Mystery", Parsons, Kansas, <u>Sun</u>, June 9, to August 11, 1934, inclusive

Hosfelt, Toddy, "Bender Day at the Cherryvale Museum", Cherryvale <u>Gazette</u>, October 15, 1989

Matlock, Kristi, "Bender Story to Air", <u>Cherryvale Citizen</u>, October 14, 1987

McKinney, Roger, "Vantage Point Highest in County", Parsons <u>Sun</u>, October 24, 1990

Parsons, Kansas, <u>Sun</u>, June 17, 1871, to September 13, 1873, inclusive

"The Cherryvale Murders", Leavenworth, Kansas, <u>Daily Times</u>, May 11, 1873

"The Bloody Benders", <u>The Tulsa Tribune</u>, September 14, 1977

Whitten, Laurie, "Inn Draws From the Past", Parsons <u>Sun</u>, 1988

"Worst Mass Murderers", Kansas City <u>Star</u>, 1989

LOCALLY PRINTED RESOURCES

Augustine, Anita, <u>The Benders and Their Legend</u>

Brigden, Bruce, "The Bloody Benders", Cherryvale Museum, Cherryvale, KS, 1966

Holland, Jim, "Have You Heard About the Benders?", song and record, 1961

Rorick, Eleanor, <u>The Notorious Benders</u>, Cherryvale Public Library, 1967

"The Bender Hills Mystery", one act play, Cherryvale Public Library, date and author unknown

DOCUMENTS AND COURT RECORDS

Court records relating to trial of Kate and Ma Bender, November 1989, to February, 1990, Labette County Courthouse, Oswego, Kansas

Highway Map of Labette County, Kansas, 1991
Land records, earliest recorded, Montgomery County Courthouse, Independence, Kansas

GRAVE MARKERS

Fawn Creek Cemetery, Montgomery County, Kansas

Harmony Grove Cemetery, Labette County, Kansas

HAND-WRITTEN LETTERS IN FILES OF CHERRYVALE MUSEUM

Botkin, George, 1960, told story of his grandfather, J.V. Wilcox and a neighbor looking for horses that had strayed away. Stopped for dinner at the Benders, and refused to sit with backs to the canvas as asked to do. Instead, they sat facing each other, and thus, no doubt saved their lives.

Carsten, Mrs. Claud, 1960, told that her grandfather, John Starkey, a preacher, stopped at Benders when returning from a cattle drive to Kansas City market, got uneasy, returned to barn on pretense of caring for horse, rode away , the two men tried to stop him.

Duncan, Mrs. Joe, 1960, great-granddaughter of Charles White, a one time sheriff of Montgomery County. A member of the posse which went after the Benders. Whenever he heard a story of some of the Benders being sighted, he would say, "No, that's not a Bender."

Langer, Elva Elma (Linn), 1960, granddaughter of Ebenezer Ester Linn. He left his wife and children at Ladore and rode away with $800 in his pocket. Reining in at the Benders, his horse reared and danced around, and the grandfather did not dismount. Included is an original poem about the Benders, written by Mrs. Langer.

Lawhead, George W., 1960, quotes his uncle, Hiram W. Lawhead, as having a claim close to the Benders, that he went to the Benders and helped dig up Mr. York and his little girl, and the Benders started to leave in a covered wagon. The uncle and others followed them to Cowskin Creek, ordered them to surrender, shooting began, and when it ended, all four Benders were dead. The men got tools and dug a grave large enough to bury all of them on the creek.

Osbourne, Wm., 1960. His uncle had been to Ft. Scott on business. Ate at the Bender place, but decided not to spend the night.

Porter, St. Elmo, December 25, 1960. He told that 70 years earlier, his uncle Tom Mortimer, took St. Elmo and the Bellamys to the corn field where the Bender Inn had stood and the outline of the "pit" was clearly visible. Where this pit had been, grew a hill of red corn. Mrs. Bellamy took an ear to show that "nothing but red corn would grow where the blood of the Bender victims was spilled."

Saller, Susanna M., January 29, 1961. Story from Bert Saller, told at 1909 burial — "Man on horseback, said to father, M.J. Saller, that he should cancel plans to go with vigilantes to Chanute to search for Benders. The man said that he belonged to the vigilantes and the Benders are cared for, so don't go to Cherokee."

Waller, Effae, October 18, 1960. Repeated usual story of crimes. Told by her uncle, Martin Van Buren Winkler.

Watts, Goldie, 1961. Said her grandfather had remarked many times, "They don't need to look for them for they won't find them. Kate fought like a tiger to the very end." Goldie's mother said that the grandfather had been part of the posse of men that had caught up with the Benders, but were not to tell who the men in the posse were. Goldie's neighbor, Mr. McComber, told her that George Loncher was his uncle and had been taking his two motherless children to his mother in Iowa, but they never reached there. Mr McComber read that it was reported that they only found the bodies of his uncle and the little girl. The other child was a boy.

PERSONAL INTERVIEWS

Foster, Dwight, (Hap), worked ground in Bender vicinity in his youth. 1991

Frease, Charlotte, grand-daughter of George Frease, who was present at discovery of bodies, and trial proceedings. 1991

Shaw, Wendell, Neosho County historian, knowledge of actual Osage Trail route, collection of pottery and china pieces from Bender Inn site. 1990

Sperry, Mildred, widow of Horace Sperry, great-nephew of Leroy Dick. 1991